Clive Oxenden Paul
with Mark Foley

English File
workbook

1

WITHOUT KEY

OXFORD
UNIVERSITY PRESS

Contents

Language practice

3	File 1	Verb *be*: present simple
9	File 2	Articles, nouns, present simple: *I / you / we / they*
14	File 3	Present simple: *he / she / it, can / can't*, the time
19	File 4	Adjectives, possessive *'s, have got,* (verb)-*ing*
24	File 5	Present simple: routines, no article, frequency
28	File 6	*There is / are*, verb *be*: past simple
33	File 7	Past simple: regular / irregular verbs
38	File 8	Present simple / continuous, future: (*be*) *going to*
42	File 9	Comparatives, predictions, countable / uncountable nouns
47	File 10	Revision / present perfect

Grammar check

49 Files 1 to 10

Read and write

59 Files 1 to 10

Listen and speak

67 Files 1 to 9

81 **Sound bank**

83 **Quicktests**

87 **Grammar words / Contractions file**

Study tip

☛ **Make a 'workfile'.**
1. Get a file.
2. Put the workbook into your file.
3. Make dividers.
4. Put notes and photocopies into your workfile after each class.

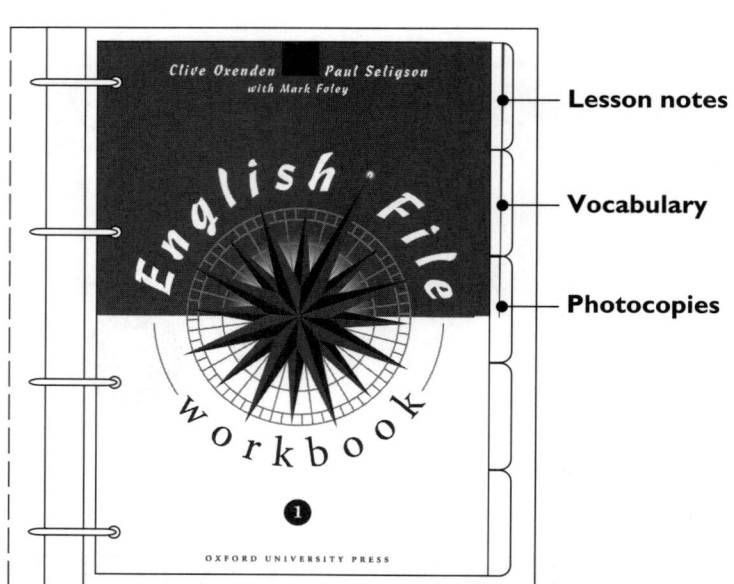

- Lesson notes
- Vocabulary
- Photocopies

> To be, or not to be – that is the question.
> William Shakespeare

Language practice 1 A

■ Verb *be*: *I / you*

1 Complete the questions and answers.

1. Excuse me. *Are you* Gary Kasparov?
   — *Yes, I am.*

2. Excuse me. *Are you* Whitney Houston?
   — *No, I'm not. I'm Janet Jackson.*
   — Sorry.

3. Excuse _me_. _Are you_ Princess Caroline?
   — Yes, _I am_.

4. _Excuse_ m_e_. _Are you_ Richard Gere?
   — No, _I'm not_. _I'm_ Mel Gibson.
   — _Sorry_.

2 Write the contractions.

1. I am Sophie. — *I'm Sophie.*
2. I am not Tarzan. — I'm not Tarzan.
3. You are Jane. — You're Jane.
4. You are not Mike. — You're not Mike.

■ Conversation

3 Match the phrases.

1. Excuse me! — d
2. Hello, I'm Mike. — e
3. Bye, see you tomorrow. — a
4. Are you Maria? — b
5. Welcome to London. — c

a Goodbye.
b Yes, I am.
c Thanks.
d Yes?
e Hi. Nice to meet you.

■ International English

4 Complete. Use a dictionary.

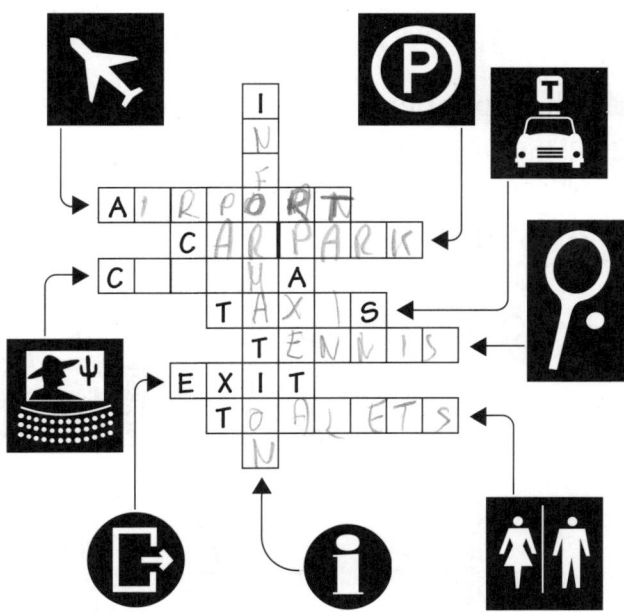

Across/Down: AIRPORT, CARPARK, CAFE, TAXIS, TENNIS, EXIT, TOILETS, INFORMATION

Words to learn

I you yes no not one two three four five
six se<u>ve</u>n eight nine ten

He<u>llo</u>. / Hi. Sorry. Thank you. / Thanks.
Goodbye. / Bye. Ex<u>cuse</u> me. Nice to meet you.
See you to<u>morr</u>ow.

1 B

My name's Bond. James Bond.
Ian Fleming

■ Instructions

1 Match the words and pictures.

a Complete   5
b Listen   1
c Write   6
d Match   4
e Say   2
f Repeat   3

■ The alphabet

2 Complete the pronunciation chart with the letters.

R W I H C M D V S K

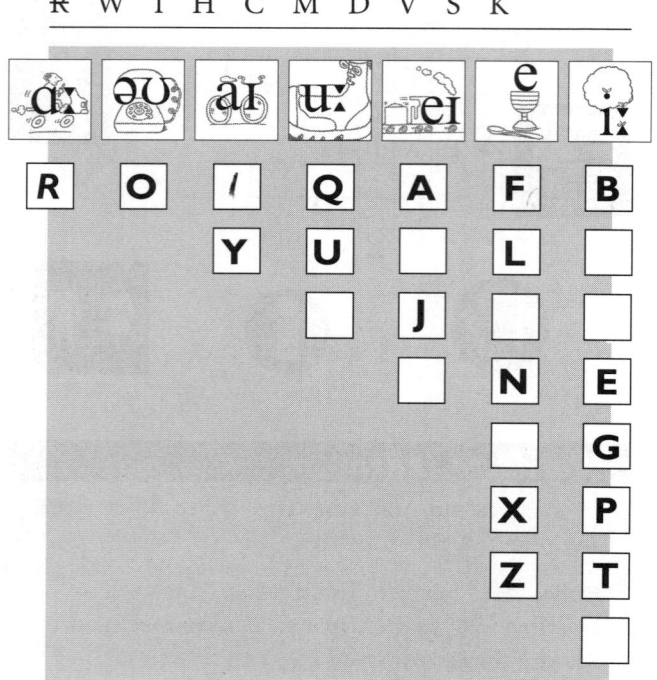

■ I / you / my / your

3 **a** Complete the dialogue.

RECEPTIONIST Good afternoon. What's
¹ *your* name?
KAREL ² My name's Offerman.
RECEPTIONIST Sorry? How do ³ you spell it?
KAREL O-F-F-E-R-M-A-N.
RECEPTIONIST And what's ⁴ your first name?
KAREL Karel.
RECEPTIONIST Where are ⁵ you from, Karel?
KAREL ⁶ I'm from Holland.
RECEPTIONIST Are ⁷ you from Amsterdam?
KAREL Yes, ⁸ I am.

b Complete the student card.

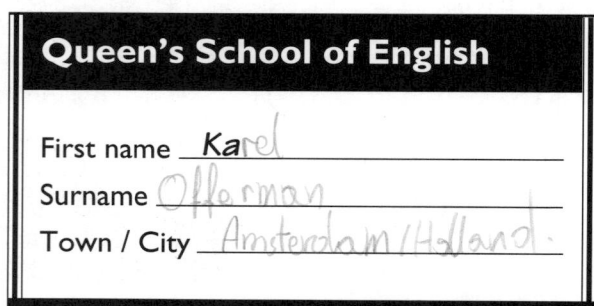

Queen's School of English

First name Karel
Surname   Offerman
Town / City Amsterdam/Holland

Words to learn

my   your   first name   surname   room
capital / double / small letter (of the alphabet)
What?   Where?   How?

What's your name?   Where are you from?
How do you spell it?   That's right.
Good morning / afternoon / evening.   Goodnight.

1 C

■ Questions

1 Write the questions.

1 's name his what ?
   What's his name?

2 she from where 's ?
   Where's she from?

3 is American Susan ?
   Susane is american?

4 from you where are ?
   Where are you from?

5 name her what 's ?
   Whats her name?

6 German is she ?
   Is she German?

■ he's / she's / his / her

2 Complete the sentences for photos 1 to 4.

1 *His* name's Pedro. *He's* from Lisbon. *He's* Portuguese.

2 _My_ name's Anna. _I'm_ from Hamburg. _I'm_ German.

3 _Her_ name's Valentina. _Her_ from St Petersburg. _____ Russian.

4 _____ name's Mehmet. _____ from Istanbul. _____ Turkish.

Words to learn

he   she   his   her   man   wo<u>m</u>an   <u>fa</u>mous   in   <u>coun</u>try   natio<u>nal</u>ity   Who?

I don't know.

● **Student's Book** Learn ♪ **Countries and nationalities** *p.132*.

■ Negatives

3 Write the answers for photos 5 to 8.

5 Is he American?
   No, he isn't. He's Swedish.

6 Is she Hungarian?
   _____ Greek.

7 Is he Mexican?
   _____ Spanish.

8 Is she British?
   _____ French.

■ Countries

4 a Write the countries for photos 1 to 8.

   b <u>Underline</u> the stress.

T_____

S_____

G_____

Portugal

G_____

R_____

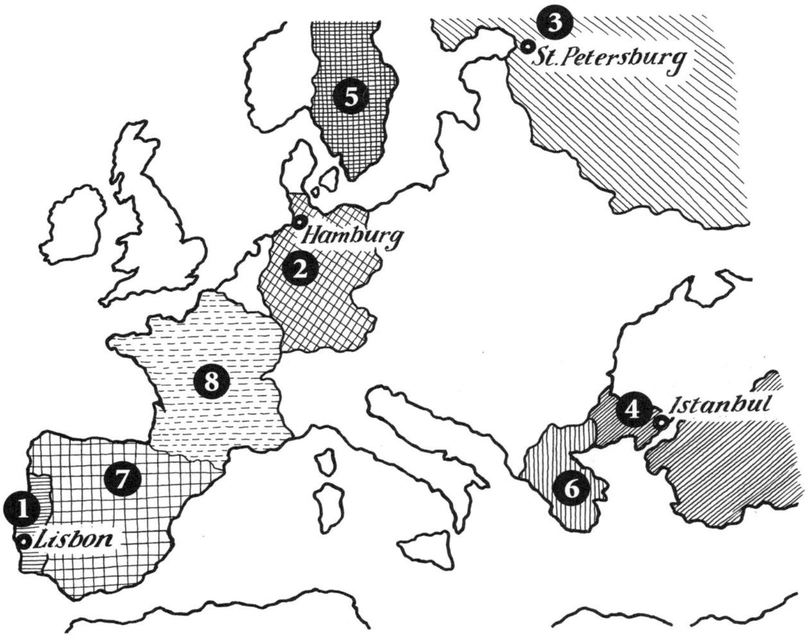

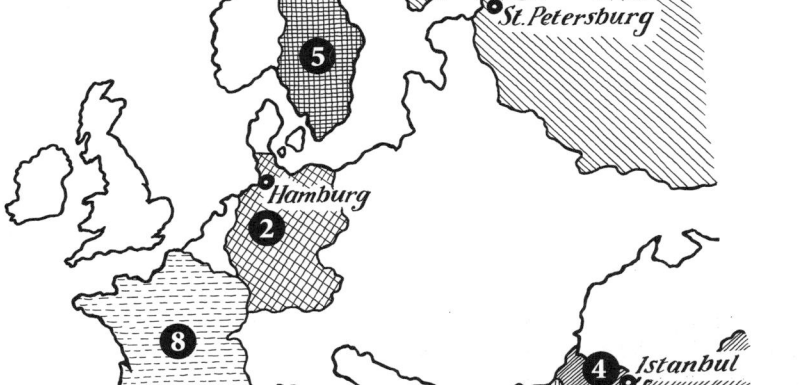

S_____

F_____

1 D

Mr Watson, come here.
Alexander Graham Bell

■ Phone numbers

1 Match the words and numbers.

1. double seven nine six four eight — *d*
2. three double oh five two one — *b*
3. three oh five two double one — *a*
4. double seven nine five eight six — *f*
5. three oh two five double two — *c*
6. seven nine double six four eight — *e*

| a 305211 | c 302522 | e 796648 |
| b 300521 | d 779648 | f 779586 |

■ Verb *be*: *he / she / it*

2 Complete the dialogues.

1. *Is* he American? Yes, *he* is.
2. Is *it* a hospital? No, it *isn't*. It's a hotel.
3. Is _____ a TV? No, _____ isn't. It _____ a computer.
4. _____ it Japanese? Yes, _____ _____ .
5. _____ she a doctor? No, _____ isn't. _____ a teacher.
6. Is your car German? No, _____ _____ . _____ Italian.

■ Punctuation

3 Punctuate the sentences.

1. is she french — *Is she French?*
2. its brazilian — _____
3. whats your name — _____
4. wheres she from — _____
5. my names vito — _____
6. im from italy — _____

■ Imperatives

4 Match the pictures and phrases. Use a dictionary.

A **Don't walk.** ☐
B **Please don't smoke.** ☐
C **Please pay here.** ☐
D *Please don't talk.* [2]
E Read the instructions. ☐

■ Classroom language

5 **a** Write the sentences.

1. don't know I
   I don't know.
2. this what's English in ?
   _____
3. remember don't I
   _____
4. spell you it do how ?
   _____
5. you it do how pronounce ?
   _____

b Translate and learn the phrases.

Words to learn

<u>o</u>pen ©lose come stop bag book ca<u>ss</u>ette chair desk <u>d</u>ictionary door file <u>p</u>aper pen pen<u>c</u>il <u>v</u>ideo <u>w</u>indow phone <u>n</u>umber it a please

● Circle six words with the sound k .

The best things in life are free.
English proverb

1 E

■ Instructions

1 Match the words and pictures.

1 Ask [D]   3 Read ☐   5 <u>Number</u> ☐
2 Spell ☐   4 <u>Circle</u> ☐   6 Under<u>line</u> ☐

■ Vocabulary groups

2 Complete.

1 two, four, six, *eight*, ten
2 Sunday, Saturday, Friday, _____, Wednesday
3 twenty-one, twenty, nineteen, eighteen, _____, sixteen
4 twenty-two, twenty-four, _____, twenty-eight
5 three, six, nine, _____, fifteen

■ Verb *be*: *we / you / they*

3 Write the plural.

Singular	Plural

1 She's Egyptian.	*They're Egyptian.*
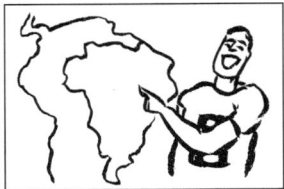	
2 He's from Brazil.	They're from Brazil.

3 I'm Chinese.	We're Chinese

4 You're in room 29.   You're in room 29.

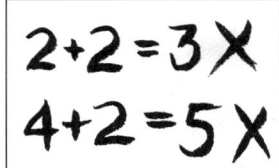

5 It's wrong. _____

■ Negatives

4 Write the negatives.

1 She's British.   *She isn't British.*
2 We're free.   _____
3 You're right.   _____
4 It's Friday.   _____
5 They're very good. _____
6 I'm Turkish.   _____

■ Questions and answers

5 Complete the dialogues.

1 *Is* it Wednesday tomorrow? Yes, it _____ .
2 _____ you Mexican? Yes, we _____ .
3 _____ General Motors and Ford Japanese? No, they _____ . They _____ American.
4 Where _____ you from? We _____ from Canada.
5 _____ you from Montreal? No, we _____ . _____ from Quebec.

Words to learn

<u>Mo</u>nday <u>Tues</u>day <u>Wed</u>nesday <u>Thurs</u>day
<u>Fri</u>day <u>Sat</u>urday <u>Sun</u>day seat we they
When?

I speak German.   See you on Wednesday.
Don't worry.

• <u>Underline</u> the stress.
• **Student's Book** Learn **Numbers A** *p.132*.

1 TRAVEL WITH ENGLISH

> About a billion people in the world use English to communicate.
> *The Guinness Book of Records*

■ Conversation

1 **a** Match the dialogues and pictures A to F.

1. Landing cards?
   Yes, please. Do you have a pen?
   Yes, here you are.
   Picture D

2. Passports, please.
   Here you are.
   Thank you. Welcome to the UK.
   Picture F

3. Smoking or non-smoking?
   Non-smoking, _pleas_.
   Seats 12B and 12C. Here you are.
   Picture B

4. Anything to drink, sir?
   No, thanks. Nothing for me.
   And for you, madam?
   Orange juice with ice, please.
   Thank you very much.
   Here you are.
   Picture C

5. Goodbye.
   Thanks. Bye.
   Goodbye, sir.
   Picture A

6. Good morning.
   Hello.
   Seat numbers 12B and C. Here. Thank you.
   Picture ☐

b Complete dialogues 2 to 4 with the phrases.

Thank you.   You're welcome.   please

■ Drinks

2 What are the drinks? <u>Underline</u> the stress.

1. LARINME TAREW
   <u>mineral</u> <u>water</u>

2. ANROEG CIJEU
   _____

3. TAE IWHT LIKM
   _____

4. CLABK OCEEFF HTWI RAGSU
   _____

5. EKCO WHTI CEI DAN NOLEM
   _____

Words to learn

<u>coffee</u> <u>coke</u> ice <u>lemon</u> milk <u>orange</u> juice
<u>sugar</u> tea <u>water</u> plane and with

- (Circle) one word with the sound .

- **Student's Book** Learn 🧳 **Travel phrasebook 1** p.130.

Politics is not a science but ... an art.
Prince Otto von Bismarck

2 A

■ Articles

1 Write *a* or *an*.

1. *an* answer
2. *a* bus
3. _____ city
4. _____ match
5. _____ key
6. _____ country
7. _____ umbrella
8. _____ dictionary
9. _____ address

■ Plurals

2 Write the nouns from exercise 1 in the right group.

Spelling		
+ -s	+ -es	consonant + y = -ies
answers	buses	cities
_____	_____	_____
_____	_____	_____

■ What's this? / What are these?

3 Write questions and answers.

1.  What's *this*?
   It's *a credit card*.

2.  What are *these*?
   They're *stamps*.

3.  What's _____?
   It's _____.

4.  What are _____?
   They're _____.

5. _____
   _____

6. _____
   _____

■ Numbers

4 Write the next number.

1. thirty, forty, *fifty*
2. ninety, eighty, _____
3. ninety-nine, a hundred, _____
4. forty-one, fifty-two, _____
5. seventy-six, sixty-five, _____

Study tip

☛ **Compare English with your language. Complete the chart.**

Chinese has thousands of characters. The Russian alphabet has 32 letters, Turkish has 29, and Arabic has 28. What about English and your language?

How many ...?	English	Your language
letters	26	
vowels (aeiou)	5	
consonants (bcd, etc.)	21	

Words to learn

a / an   this   these   <u>add</u>ress   case   <u>pock</u>et
um<u>brel</u>la   <u>vow</u>el   <u>con</u>sonant   How <u>man</u>y?

- (Circle) the word with the sound  |eɪ|.

- **Student's Book** Learn ♫ **Numbers B** *p.132* and ♫ **Small objects** *p.134*.

2 B

> Television is chewing gum for the eyes.
> *Frank Lloyd Wright*

■ Nouns

1 Write the words.

1 *the door*
2 *the shelves*
3 the table
4 picture
5 clock
6 bin
7 floor
8 _____
9 _____
10 _____

■ Prepositions

2 Write questions and answers.

1 Where's the bin?
   It's on the floor.
2 *Where are the papers?*
   They're in the bin.
3 Where's the chair?
   _____ desk.
4 _____ pictures?
   They're next to the clock.
5 Where are the files?
   _____
6 _____?
   They're in the door.
7 Where's the fax?
   _____ computer.

■ Plurals

3 Complete the chart.

Singular	Plural
1 Where's the key?	*Where are the keys?*
2 What's that?	
3 Is this your bag?	
4 It isn't very nice.	
5 Open the window.	
6 That's my book.	

■ Pronunciation

4 (Circle) the plural with the ending /ɪz/.

1 trees (witches) books
2 cameras keys oranges
3 notebooks glasses toilets
4 days buses pairs
5 cases cassettes wallets

Words to learn

the that those here there put in on
next to under bin drawer shelf (*pl.* shelves)
floor wall office

● (Circle) three words with the sound .

10

> I want to be alone.
> *Greta Garbo*

2 C

■ Present simple: *I / you / we / they*

1 Complete the sentences with a word from the list.

~~quite~~   a   well   don't

1. I speak Turkish *quite* well.
2. I speak Greek very _____ .
3. We speak _____ little Portuguese.
4. They _____ speak Swedish.

2 **a** Write the questions.

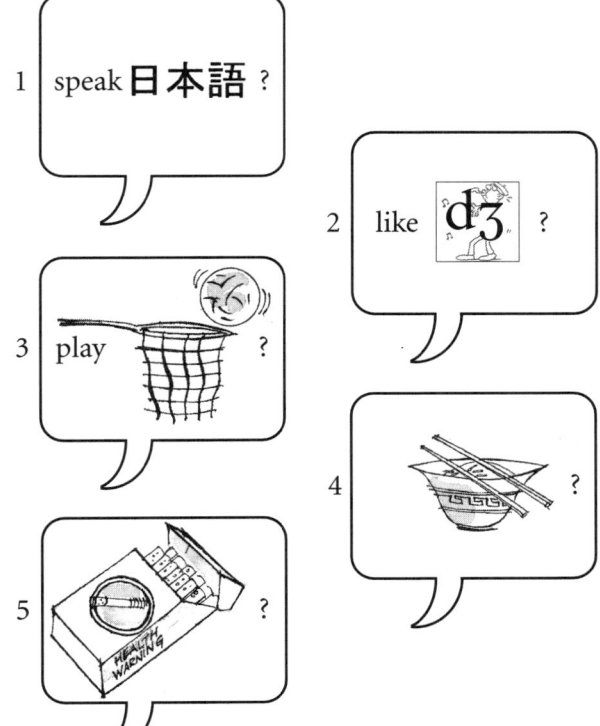

	Question	Your answer
1	*Do you speak Japanese?*	_____
2	_____	_____
3	_____	_____
4	_____	_____
5	_____	_____

b Write *your* answers: *Yes, I do.* or *No, I don't.*

3 Complete the chart.

	+	−
1	We *understand*.	We *don't understand*.
2	They play tennis.	They _____ tennis.
3	You _____ Angela.	You don't know Angela.
4	We study history.	We _____ history.
5	I _____ fast food.	I don't like fast food.

■ Writing

4 Write *and*, *but*, or *or*.

1. I speak French *and* English, _____ I don't speak German.
2. They don't want tea _____ coffee.
3. We play volleyball _____ we don't play football.
4. I like mineral water _____ orange juice, _____ I don't like milk _____ coke.

■ Pronunciation

5 Put the words in the right group.

~~don't~~   ~~we~~   ~~two~~   ~~five~~   three   my   go
speak   know   do   like   food

 iː	 uː	 əʊ	 aɪ
we	two	don't	five
___	___	___	___

Words to learn

know   like   play   smoke   <u>study</u>   want (to)
food   music   a <u>little</u>   but   or   (quite) well

- (Circle) two words with the sound .

- **Student's Book** Learn 🔖 **Languages** *p.132* and 🔖 **Food and drink A** *p.135*.

2 D

> Remember that time is money.
> *Benjamin Franklin*

■ Jobs

1 Write sentences. Use the jobs in the list.

a secretary   ~~a teacher~~   doctors
a shop assistant   journalists   ~~pilots~~
a waiter   students

1 I work in a school. *I'm a teacher.*
2 They fly planes. *They're pilots.*
3 I work in a restaurant. _____
4 We work in a hospital. _____
5 They work for a newspaper. _____
   _____
6 I work in an office. _____
7 They study at university. _____
   _____
8 I work in a shop. _____

■ Articles

2 Write *a*, *an*, or (–).

1 We're __–__ engineers.
2 I'm _____ engineer.
3 It's _____ identity card.
4 Do you have _____ pen, please?
5 They work in _____ office.
6 I like _____ American cigarettes.

■ Conversation

3 Match the questions and answers.

1 Are you a student? | *c*
2 What do you do? | ☐
3 Where do you work? | ☐
4 Do you like it? | ☐
5 What languages do you speak? | ☐
6 Do you smoke? | ☐

a Yes, I do. It's a good job.
b I'm a nurse.
c No, I'm not.
d In a hospital, in Bath.
e No, I don't.
f Portuguese and English.

■ Ordinal numbers

4 **a** Complete the chart.

+ -th	Different spelling
four → *fourth*	one → first
six → _____	_____ → second
seven → _____	_____ → third
ten → _____	_____ → fifth
	_____ → eighth
	_____ → ninth

b Do the quiz.

1 If Sunday is the *seventh* day of the week, Thursday is the _____ .
2 Neil Armstrong: the _____ man on the moon.
3 C is the _____ letter of the alphabet.
4 This is the _____ File in this book.

Words to learn

<u>lawyer</u>   journalist   <u>racing</u> <u>driver</u>   high   low
<u>salary</u>   stress   course   work (*v.*)

What do you do? = What's your job?

- Circle two words with the sound .

- **Student's Book** Learn 🕮 **Time A** *p.136* and 🕮 **Jobs** *p.137.*

12

When a man is tired of London, he is tired of life.
Samuel Johnson

TRAVEL WITH ENGLISH   2

■ Conversation

1   Complete the dialogues with the phrases.

Can I have a tuna salad and a coke, please?
Thanks very much.   Do you have a pen?
Can I change $100, please?   ~~Good morning~~.
Yes, here you are.   How much is that?

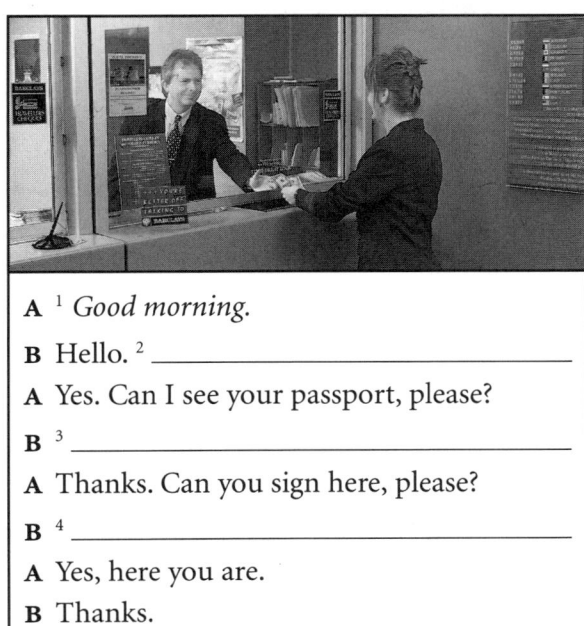

A ¹ *Good morning.*
B Hello. ² _____
A Yes. Can I see your passport, please?
B ³ _____
A Thanks. Can you sign here, please?
B ⁴ _____
A Yes, here you are.
B Thanks.

A Hi. ⁵ _____
B Anything else?
A No, thanks. ⁶ _____
B £5.50, please.
A Here you are.
B Thank you. Have a nice day.
A ⁷ _____

Words to learn

apple   pizza   salad   tuna   regular   large
exchange   rate   today   How much?

Have a nice day.

- (Circle) two words with the sound .

- **Student's Book** Learn 📖 Travel phrasebook 2 p.130.

■ Food and drink

2   Write the food on the menu.

■ Prices

3 [a] Punctuate each question.

1 canihaveacheeseburgerandacoffeeplease
   Can I have _____
   That's $13.50, please.

2 threetunasaladsalargecokeandtwoteasplease
   _____
   That's $_____ , please.

3 canihavealargepizzaandaregularcoke
   withiceplease
   _____
   That's $_____ , please.

[b] How much is it?

3 A

Present simple: *he / she*

1 Write sentences.

+

1 I read *Time* magazine. (he / *Newsweek*)
   He reads Newsweek.

2 We live in a house. (she / flat)
   _____

3 They watch CNN. (Ben / MTV)
   _____

4 You study geography (Erica / history)
   _____

5 I have tea in the morning. (Jo / coffee)
   _____

−

6 You don't like football. (he / tennis)
   He doesn't like tennis.

7 We don't speak Polish. (Anna / Italian)
   _____

8 I don't want a drink. (she / sandwich)
   _____

9 I don't work in the evenings. (she / afternoons)
   _____

Short answers

Focus on Hong Kong

My name's Lee Hung Suk. I'm twenty-one. I live with my family in a small flat in Hong Kong. I study psychology. I speak English and Chinese. I like Chinese and Italian food. I don't drink coffee or milk but I love Chinese tea. I don't smoke and I don't have a car. In the evenings, I watch TV or films on video. On Saturdays, I go to discos and on Sundays, I play basketball or table tennis.

2 Complete the questions and answers.

1 *Does* Lee live in a flat?   Yes, *he does.*

2 _____ he work?   No, *he doesn't*. He *studies* psychology.

3 _____ he speak Chinese?   Yes, _____ .

4 _____ he drink milk?   _____ , he _____ . He _____ tea.

5 _____ a car?   _____ , he _____ .

6 _____ study on Saturdays?   No, _____ . He _____ discos.

Writing

3 Write about Lee.

His name's Lee Hung Suk. He's twenty-one. He lives …

Verb: *have*

4 **a** Complete with *have* or *has*.

1 *Have* a nice day!

2 He _____ a cat but he doesn't _____ a dog.

3 Do you _____ coffee for breakfast?

4 She _____ fish and chips on Fridays.

5 Can I _____ a photocopy, please?

b Translate the sentences. How many different verbs do you use for *have* in your language? ☐

Words to learn

go (to)   have (= eat or drink)   live   read
watch (*v.*)   after   house/flat   children
newspaper

• Circle three words with the sound .

Life begins at forty.
English proverb

3 B

■ Verb phrases

1 Complete the phrases with the words.

magazine ~~volleyball~~ piano picture
Barcelona horse children French food

1 play *volleyball*
2 play the _____
3 eat _____
4 have two _____
5 read a _____
6 paint a _____
7 live in _____
8 ride a _____

■ Questions and answers

2 **a** Complete his questions.

1 Where *do you live*, Miss Spencer?
   I live in Chelsea.
2 What _____?
   I'm a lawyer.
3 What languages _____?
   French and a little Greek.
4 What kind of music _____?
   I like opera and classical music.
5 And what sports _____?
   I play golf and tennis.

PERFECT PARTNERS
AGENCY

NAME *Harry Gordon*
AGE *22*
ADDRESS *78 Blackmore Road,*
Hackney, London E8
JOB *Disc jockey*
LANGUAGES *Italian*
SPORTS *football, basketball*
MUSIC *disco and rock*

b Read Harry's form. Complete the dialogue.

AGENT Harry Gordon is the perfect partner for you!
ELIZABETH Really? What ¹ *does* he do?
AGENT He ² _____ a disc jockey.
ELIZABETH ³ _____ does he ⁴ _____ ?
AGENT He ⁵ _____ in Hackney.
ELIZABETH ⁶ _____ languages ⁷ _____ he ⁸ _____ ?
AGENT He ⁹ _____ Italian.
ELIZABETH ¹⁰ _____ he play tennis?
AGENT No, he ¹¹ _____ . He ¹² _____ football and basketball.
ELIZABETH What ¹³ _____ of music ¹⁴ _____ he like?
AGENT He ¹⁵ _____ disco and rock.
ELIZABETH Oh, dear. Are you sure he's my perfect partner?

Words to learn

drive   paint *a picture*   play *the cello*   ride
maga<u>z</u>ine   TV <u>programme</u>   <u>a</u>ll   be<u>fore</u>
What kind of …?

● (Circle) three words with the sound .

3 C

> You can't make an omelette without breaking eggs.
> *Robert Louis Stevenson*

■ can / can't

1 Write a sentence for each picture.

1 *They can't make an omelette.*
2 _____
3 _____
4 _____
5 _____

2 **a** Write a question for each picture.

                              Your answer

1 *Can* you *make an omelette?* _____
2 ___ you _____ ? _____
3 ___ you _____ ? _____
4 ___ you _____ ? _____
5 ___ you _____ ? _____

b Write your answer: *Yes, I can.* or *No, I can't.*

3 **a** Write the sentences.

1 cook well quite can we *We can cook quite well.*
2 here smoke I can ?
    _____
3 guitar play you can the ?
    _____
4 can't well she play very chess
    _____
5 phone you I use can your ?
    _____

b Translate the sentences.

■ Pronunciation

4 Put the words in the right group.

~~act~~ ~~are~~ bank can can't class flat
large park stand start thanks

æ	ɑː
act	are
___	___
___	___
___	___
___	___
___	___

Words to learn

act do <u>some</u>thing help j<u>ug</u>gle sing pi<u>a</u>no
show (*n.*)

That's e<u>nough</u>.

- (Circle) three words with the sound  .

- **Student's Book** Learn Verbs A *p.139*.

16

> When it's three o'clock in New York, it's still 1938 in London.
> *Bette Midler*

3 D

■ What's the time?

1 Draw the clocks.

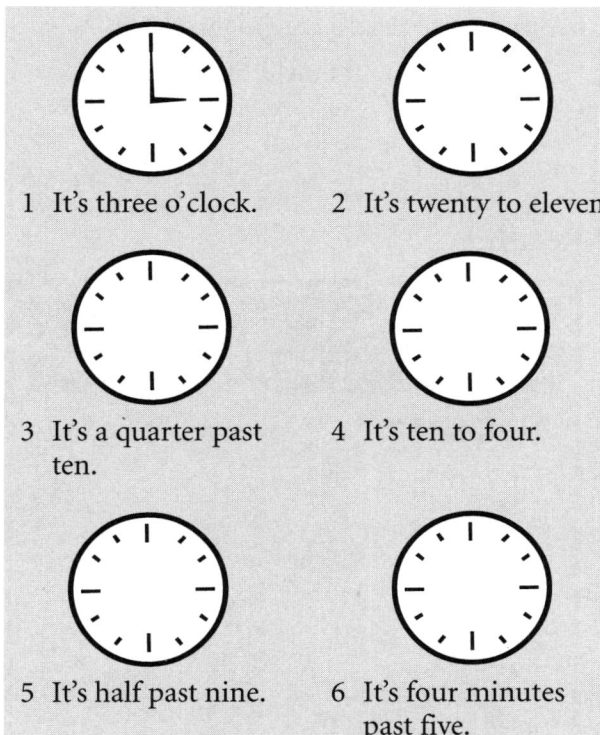

1 It's three o'clock. 2 It's twenty to eleven.
3 It's a quarter past ten. 4 It's ten to four.
5 It's half past nine. 6 It's four minutes past five.

2 Write the times.

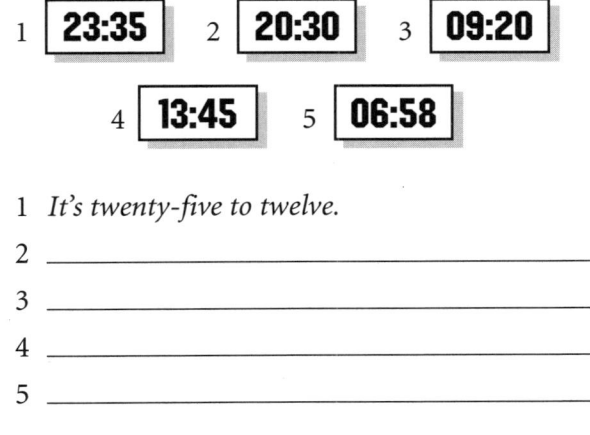

1 *It's twenty-five to twelve.*
2 _____
3 _____
4 _____
5 _____

3 Complete and draw the times.

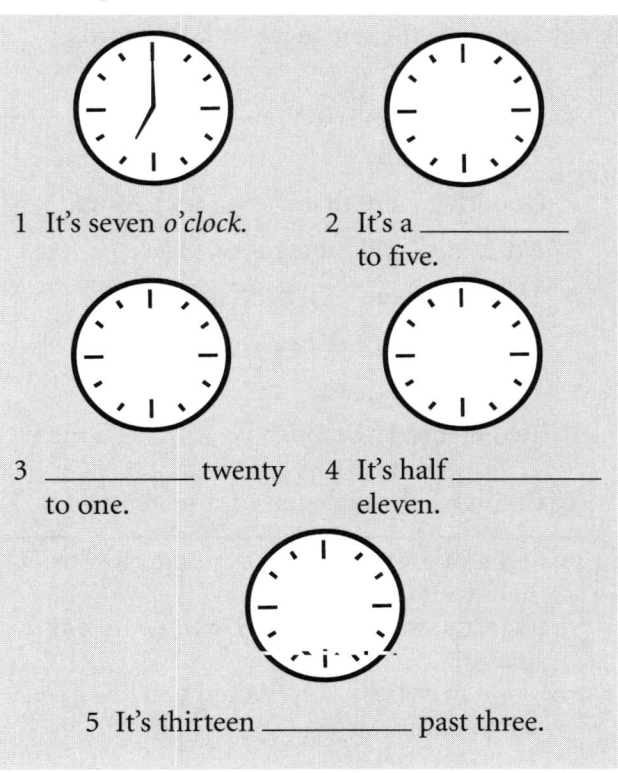

1 It's seven *o'clock*.   2 It's a _____ to five.
3 _____ twenty to one.   4 It's half _____ eleven.
5 It's thirteen _____ past three.

■ Time words

4 Write the missing word.

1 Saturday / day   July / *month*
2 day / week   month / _____
3 12.00 / midday   24.00 / _____
4 60 seconds / minute   60 minutes / _____
5 thirty / half   fifteen / _____
6 the morning / in   night / _____

■ Adjectives

5 Match the problems and answers.

1 I'm tired.   [d]
2 We're hungry.   [ ]
3 She's hot.   [ ]
4 I'm cold.   [ ]
5 We're thirsty.   [ ]
6 We're very late. [ ]

a Have my jacket.
b Have a drink.
c Have a sandwich.
d Have a black coffee.
e OK. Let's go.
f Open the window.

Words to learn

<u>se</u>cond <u>mi</u>nute hour day month year
<u>qu</u>arter half past / to at mid<u>d</u>ay / <u>mi</u>dnight

What's the time?   It's two o'clock.

- (Circle) two words with the sound .

- **Student's Book** Learn 🎵 Time B *p.136*.

3 TRAVEL WITH ENGLISH

> Hollywood is a great place ... if you're an orange.
> *Fred Allen*

■ Conversation

1 **a** Complete the sentences with the words.

have ~~is~~ you the it a much

1 Without *is* fine.
2 Goodnight and thank you very _much_.
3 No, _____ double room, please.
4 Thanks. Where's _____ lift?
5 Hello. Do you _have_ any rooms?
6 Here _you_ are.
7 Two nights. How much is _____ a night?

b Complete the dialogue with sentences 1 to 7.

RECEPTIONIST	Good evening. How can I help you?
BUSINESSMAN	¹ *Hello. Do you have any rooms?*
RECEPTIONIST	Yes. Would you like a single room, sir?
BUSINESSMAN	² _____
RECEPTIONIST	With or without a bathroom?
BUSINESSMAN	³ _____
RECEPTIONIST	Fine. How many nights would you like to stay?
BUSINESSMAN	⁴ _____
RECEPTIONIST	It's fifty-five dollars a night, including breakfast. Can I see your passport, please?
BUSINESSMAN	⁵ _____
RECEPTIONIST	Thank you. Room 403 on the fourth floor. Here's your key.
BUSINESSMAN	⁶ _____
RECEPTIONIST	It's over there, next to the stairs. Goodnight, sir.
BUSINESSMAN	⁷ _____

c Complete with *one* word.

He wants a ¹ *double* room ² _____ a bathroom for ³ _____ nights. It's ⁴ $_____ a night including ⁵ _____. He's in room ⁶ _____ on the ⁷ _____ floor.

■ Reading

```
JET TRAVEL
ONLINE RESERVATIONS

Singapore

001
Hyatt Regency
single rooms $150 per night + 10% tax;
double rooms $195 + 10% tax.

002
Lion City
single rooms $100;
double rooms $170 per night.
No taxes.

003
New Park
single rooms $105 + 10% tax;
double rooms $150 +10% tax.
```

2 Read the list. Which hotel can you stay in?

a You're married. You're with your partner in Singapore. You want to stay for three nights. You have $500. _____

b You're on holiday with some friends. You want to stay in Singapore for two nights. You want three single rooms. You have $650. _____

Words to learn

bath shower lift with without

It's on the first / second floor.

- ⓒircle two words with the sound .

- **Student's Book** Learn 🧳 **Travel phrasebook 3** p.130.

I'm young, I'm fast, I'm pretty.
Muhammad Ali

4 A

■ Adjectives

1 Write another sentence. Use the opposite adjective.

1 Jane's rich.
   She *isn't poor*.
2 The Porsche 922 isn't slow.
   It's _____.
3 Mr and Mrs Jensen are short.
   They _____.
4 Burgers and pizzas are cheap.
   They _____.
5 Mr Universe isn't weak.
   He _____.

2 Write sentences.

1 *She's a good actress.* 2 *They're sad faces.*

3 _____ 4 _____

5 _____ 6 _____

■ Colours

3 Write the colours.

1 red + white = *pink*
2 blue + yellow = _____
3 black + white = _____
4 blue + red = _____
5 red + blue + yellow = _____

■ Reading

4

Words to learn

black blue brown green grey <u>o</u>range
pink <u>pu</u>rple red white <u>ye</u>llow <u>fu</u>nny
<u>a</u>bout *40 years old* good-<u>loo</u>king
What <u>co</u>lour ...?

• (Circle) seven words with the sound .

• **Student's Book** Learn ▰ **Adjectives** *p.140*.

4 B

> I want to be the white man's brother, not his brother-in-law.
> *Martin Luther King*

■ Family and possessive 's

1 Complete.

1 Who's your mother's sister? *My aunt.*
2 Who's your *grandmother's* husband? My grandfather.
3 Who's your father's _____ ? My uncle.
4 Who's your _____ wife? My mother.
5 Who's your son's _____ ? My daughter.
6 Who's your nephew's sister? My _____ .

Words to learn

aunt brother child (*pl.* children) daughter
father family friend husband man (*pl.* men)
nephew niece (grand)parents
person (*pl.* people) sister son uncle
wife (*pl.* wives) woman (*pl.* women) our their

- (Circle) eight female words.

2 Write one ' in each phrase.

1 Beethoven's fifth symphony.
2 McDonalds restaurants.
3 Look at the Students Book.
4 Todays exchange rates.
5 Shakespeares plays.

■ Writing

3 **a** Read paragraph 1. Name the people in the photo A to D.

b Write paragraph 1 again. Use the words in the list, not the underlined names.

their they they his

c Complete paragraphs 2 and 3. Use the words in the lists. Check for capital letters.

her his it their (paragraph 2)

her she they our (paragraph 3)

A Family Business

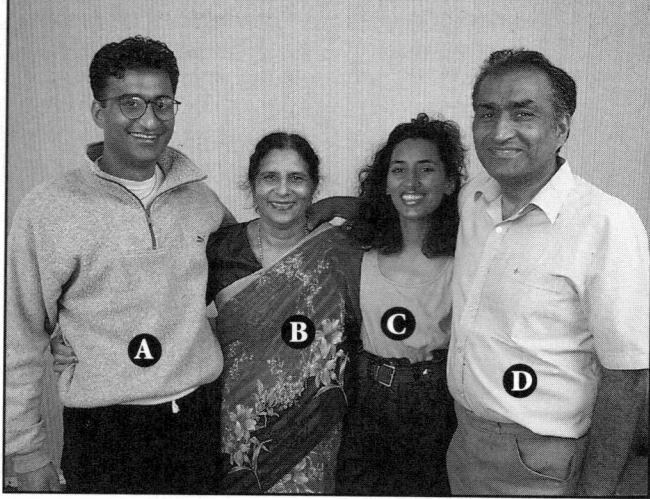

Ⓐ _____   **Ⓒ** Usha Mehta
Ⓑ _____   **Ⓓ** _____

1 Sanjay Mehta is from Bombay, in India. ¹ <u>Sanjay's</u> wife, Meena, is from Srinagar. But now ² <u>Sanjay and Meena</u> live in Bradford, in the north of England, with ³ <u>Sanjay and Meena's</u> two children, Kumar and Usha. ⁴ <u>Sanjay and Meena</u> have a small shop.

2 ⁵ _____ shop's in the centre of Bradford. ⁶ _____ opens from eight a.m. to ten p.m. Meena and ⁷ _____ husband work there all day, and the children help after school. Sometimes Kumar does ⁸ _____ homework in the shop.

3 When the children are in the shop Meena goes upstairs and makes the dinner. ⁹ _____ usually cooks Indian food for ¹⁰ _____ family. The Mehta family aren't rich but ¹¹ _____ like their life in Bradford and don't want to go back to India. ' ¹² _____ home now is here in Bradford,' says Sanjay.

I've got nothing to declare except my genius.
Oscar Wilde

4 C

Reading

1 Read and complete. Use a dictionary.

Here are some facts about the world's population:

- 36% are under 15 years old
- 6% are over 65 years old
- 20% have got a radio
- 5% have got a car
- 7% have got a TV
- 60% haven't got clean drinking water
- 25% haven't got enough to eat
- 8% are unemployed

(from Earth Facts, 1990)

1 How many people *have got* clean drinking water? *Forty per cent.*

2 How many people *haven't* got a job?
_____

3 How many people haven't got _____ TV?
_____

4 How many _____ are between fifteen and sixty-five years old? _____

5 How many people _____ enough to _____ ? Twenty-five per cent.

have / has got

2 **a** Complete the questions with *Have* or *Has*.

1 *Has* your car got electric windows? [c]
2 _____ they got a nice house? [ ]
3 _____ she got a new car? [ ]
4 _____ you got an umbrella? [ ]
5 _____ we got any sandwiches? [ ]
6 _____ he got a good stereo? [ ]

a No, I haven't.
b No, she's got an old Peugeot 205.
c Yes, and it's very fast.
d Yes, it's got a lovely garden.
e Yes, he has. He's got a Sony.
f No, but we've got some biscuits.

b Match the questions and answers.

have got + a / some / any

3 Complete the sentences. Use contractions.

1 They*'ve* got *some* beautiful paintings.
2 My brother *has*n't got *any* children.
3 _____ you got _____ matches?
4 I _____ got _____ new boots.
5 _____ James got _____ good job?
6 She _____n't got _____ sisters.
7 Katerina _____ got four children and _____ small flat.
8 They _____ got _____ fast car and _____ lot of money but they _____n't got _____ friends.
9 We _____ got _____ letters and _____ envelopes but we _____n't got _____ stamps.

4 Complete **Contractions file A** *p.87*.

Words to learn

<u>d</u>ivorced   <u>n</u>atural   poor   professional
rich   <u>i</u>dea   <u>m</u>icrowave   <u>p</u>roblem   a lot of
<u>m</u>oney   some   <u>a</u>ny

- (Circle) three words with the sound .

21

4 D

> I'm not a vegetarian because I love animals; I'm a vegetarian because I hate plants.
> A. Whitney Brown

■ Spelling: (verb)-ing

1 Put the verbs in the right spelling group.

~~swim~~ ~~cycle~~ ~~garden~~ ski shop run
study write drive ride paint

No change	Spelling change	
+ -ing	Double final consonant	–e + -ing
garden*ing*	swi*mming*	cycl*ing*
___	___	___
___	___	___
___	___	___

■ like / love / hate + (verb)-ing

2 What do Amanda and Dean like doing?

1 Amanda likes dr*inking mineral water*,
sw_____ , and re_____ ma_____ .
She loves sp_____ mo_____ , but she
hates fl_____ .

2 Dean likes *listening to* mu_____ ,
ta_____ ph_____ , and sm_____ .
He loves ea_____ ch_____ , but he
hates co_____ .

■ Revision: s or 's?

4 Complete with 's or s.

This is Alan Stewart.
¹ He's from South Africa.
² He__ got blue ³ eye__ and short blond hair.
⁴ He__ twenty-three.
⁵ He__ an international rugby player. He ⁶ love__ playing rugby. He doesn't smoke. ⁷ He__ separated, and he ⁸ live__ with his mother in a modern flat in Cape Town. ⁹ It__ very nice, and ¹⁰ it__ got a great view of the sea.
¹¹ Alan__ ex-wife Rita ¹² live__ in Johannesburg. They've got two ¹³ daughter__ .

take
cook
spend
read
~~listen to~~
eat
smoke
swim
~~drink~~
fly

music
~~mineral water~~
chocolate
magazines
photos
money

3 Write true sentences.

1 I love _____ and _____ .
2 I like _____ and _____ .
3 I don't like _____ or _____ .

Words to learn

<u>cycling</u> <u>gardening</u> <u>reading</u> <u>shopping</u> <u>skiing</u>
<u>swimming</u> <u>travelling</u> <u>walking</u> hate love
advert chess <u>hobby</u>

• (Circle) two words with the sound /æ/ .

> There are two classes of travel – first class, and with children.
> *Robert Benchley*

TRAVEL WITH ENGLISH **4**

■ Conversation

1 Match the question halves.

1 Can you — g
2 Could I —
3 How many —
4 How much —
5 Have you —
6 Do you have —
7 Do you —

a got any postcards?
b is this map?
c speak English?
d any batteries?
e bananas would you like?
f have ten stamps, please?
g give me another copy, please?

2 **a** Correct the sentences. Tick ✓ who says it.

	Assistant	Customer
1 Good morning, ~~Madam~~. (m)	✓	
2 Would you like any else?		
3 Yes, how many you like?		
4 You sell envelopes?		
5 No, thanks. How much that?		
6 £2.50, please. Thank very much.		
7 Four, please, and four stamp.		

b Write the dialogue in the right order.

A *Good morning, madam.*

Words to learn

aspirin **b**attery box **e**nvelope film market
news-stand **p**ostcard toothbrush

- Ⓒircle four words with the sound .

- **Student's Book** Revise 📖 **Places A** *p.133* and learn 🧳 **Travel phrasebook 4** *p.130*.

■ Revision

3 Do the crossword.

1Q	U	I	T	2E			3s	4
				5		6		
7		8			9			
		10				11		
						12		
13		14						
						15		
16								
					17		18	
		19		20				

Clues across →

1 I think my brother is *quite* good-looking. (5)
3 The capital of South Korea _____ Seoul. (2)
5 The opposite of *old*. (3)
7 Not cold. (3)
9 I don't _____ hamburgers. (3)
10 A hundred cents = one _____ . (6)
12 My grandfather's very _____ . (3)
14 The opposite of *sad*. (5)
15 Use *some* for ➕, use _____ for ➖ and ❓. (3)
16 I hate writing post_____ on holiday. (5)
18 I go to work _____ half-past eight. (2)
19 You can buy these at the post office. (6)

Clues down ↓

2 You put letters in these. (9)
4 Tuesday, Thursday, _____ , Monday. (8)
6 I, you, he / she / it, _____ , you, they. (2)
8 To clean your teeth, you need a _____ . (10)
11 Sweden, Belgium, Japan and Britain all have a _____ family. (5)
13 To travel on a train you need a _____ . (6)
17 Are you on holiday? Yes, I _____ . (2)
18 Can I _____ a question, please? (3)
20 Afternoon = p.m. Morning = _____ (2)

5 A

■ Reading

1 Read and match the people to one of the jobs. Use a dictionary.

dancer   farmer   nurse   postman   politician

A I go to work at ten o'clock in the evening. I wear a blue and white uniform at work. I work in a very big building with a lot of beds and windows. I like working with people. I get home at seven in the morning.

_____

B She gets up very early. She doesn't travel to work but she works outside. She works all day in the sun and rain and only stops for lunch. She finishes work at sunset.

_____

C He gets up at five o'clock in the morning and he starts work at six. He goes to work by car but at work he walks a lot. He hates dogs and he hates working when it rains! He finishes work at midday.

_____

■ Verb phrases

2 Complete the phrases with the words.

do   ~~get to~~   get up   go   go by   go to

1 *get to* work, the station
2 _____ exercise, yoga
3 _____ home, shopping
4 _____ late, at 7.30
5 _____ the cinema, a disco
6 _____ train, bus

Words to learn

do *yoga*   start / finish *work*   go to *bed*
After that / Then   early   late   healthy

How do you get to work?   It depends. / By *car*.

• (Circle) eight words with the sound .

• Learn the verbs and phrases in exercise 2.

• **Student's Book** Learn ▲ *Have, Go, Get* A *p.141*.

■ Present simple: routines

3 Read what Karen says. Then complete the interviewer's notebook.

Karen O'Connor, a New York taxi driver.

After dinner I watch TV.
I get up at seven thirty.
I finish work at five.
Then I have breakfast and go to work.
~~I have lunch at one.~~
I have dinner at seven.
I go to bed at about eleven.

Karen's Day

0730 (1) _____
0815 (2) _____
1300 (3) *She has lunch at one.*
1700 (4) _____
1900 (5) _____
2000 (6) _____
2300 (7) _____

■ Questions

4 Complete the questions about Karen.

1 *Does she* work in New York? Yes, she does.

2 What d____ s____ d____ after breakfast?
  She goes to work.

3 What time d____ s____ h____ lunch?
  At one o'clock.

4 What time d____ s____ f____ work?
  She finishes at five o'clock.

5 What d____ s____ d____ after dinner?
  She watches TV.

6 D____ s____ g____ to bed late?
  No, she doesn't.

5 B

Adverbs of frequency

1 Write sentences.

1 restaurants they have sometimes in lunch
   They sometimes have lunch in restaurants.

2 at swimming weekend we the often go
   _____

3 sleeps hours Adam a always eight night
   _____

4 early up wife never Sundays on gets my
   _____

5 food ever on hardly put I salt my
   _____

6 usually homework students their good do
   _____

Reading and dictionary work

2 **a** Read. Write the star's name.

1 *Dolly Parton* loves cooking and eating.

2 _____ doesn't eat red meat or salt and doesn't eat after dinner.

3 _____ always has breakfast, fresh food, and a lot of water.

4 _____ does a lot of exercise and doesn't eat meat or chicken.

Words to learn

break *a rule*   do *homework*   get *married*
re*cord* *your voice*   re*vise*   cup   meal   meat
salt   *vegetables*   wine   *always*   *usually*   often
sometimes   *hardly* ever   *never*   *really*

• Circle twelve words with only one syllable.

b Translate these words. Use a dictionary.

fried (*adj.*) _____   fat (*n.*) _____

herbal (*adj.*) _____   light (*adj.*) _____

c Match the phrases and meanings. Use a dictionary.

1 candy *line 2*   [c]   4 low *line 10*   [ ]
2 daily *line 5*   [ ]   5 soft drinks *line 13*   [ ]
3 seafood *line 9* [ ]   6 snacks *line 15* [ ]

a every day
b small meals, e.g. sandwiches, biscuits
c American word for sweets
d fruit juice, coke, etc.
e things you can eat from the sea
f opposite of high

How the stars stay young
Here are this week's tips:

Burt Reynolds says:

'Always eat breakfast. Don't
2 eat candy. Eat fresh fruit,
   fish, and chicken. Don't eat
4 fried food. Do exercise
   daily – walking and swimming
6 are good. And drink a lot of water!'

Kathleen Turner:

She does four hours'
8 exercise a day! Kathleen eats
   only seafood, vegetables,
10 and low-fat pasta.

Bill Cosby says:

'Eat chicken and fish.
12 Don't eat red meat! Don't
   use salt. Don't drink soft
14 drinks. Drink water and herbal tea.
   And don't have snacks after dinner!'

Dolly Parton says:

16 'I love food – I love cooking
   it and I love eating it.'
18 But Dolly usually has a
   light breakfast and lunch.
20 For dinner she has fish or
   chicken with a vegetable
22 and a salad.

5 C

The top eight prepositions in English are: *of, to, for, on, with, by, at, from.*

■ Reading

1 Write the nationalities. Use a dictionary.

International stereotypes!

A They love TV soap operas and football. Their country has a very large forest and a very long river. It has a big city with a famous beach and a big carnival once a year. These people love music and dancing, and they have parties every weekend. They drink coffee four or five times a day!

Who are they? The _____ .

B They live in a small country with a lot of mountains. They work a lot but they also love sports. They like doing sports in the winter. These people usually speak two or three languages. They're famous for their banks, their clocks, and their watches. Their national dish is cheese fondue.

Who are they? The _____ .

C They work a lot and they hardly ever have holidays. They usually go to work very early and get home very late. They've got a royal family. They're very polite and they like making things. They eat fish four or five times a week and their national dish is sushi.

Who are they? The _____ .

■ Prepositions of time

2 Complete with *at, in,* or *on.*

1 My sister starts work *at* ten o'clock _____ the evening.

2 We don't often go shopping _____ Saturday mornings.

3 I sometimes visit my grandmother _____ Sundays _____ the winter.

4 Programmes on BBC 1 usually end _____ about midnight.

5 Christmas Day is always _____ 25th December.

6 See you _____ Friday _____ half past twelve _____ the afternoon.

■ Questions

3 **a** Write the questions.

1 How often *do* you *go away* at weekends?

2 What time _____ you _____ _____ in the morning?

3 When _____ you _____ your homework?

4 How many hours _____ you _____ a day?

5 How often _____ you _____ _____ in the evenings?

b Write your answers for questions 1 to 5, e.g. *(about) once a month.*

■ Pronunciation

4 Put the words in the right groups.

~~how~~   good   full   house   road   coast   home   noun   would

aʊ	ʊ	əʊ
how	_____	_____
_____	_____	_____
_____	_____	_____

Words to learn

once / twice / three times a week / month / year
Christmas   Easter   week<u>end</u>   <u>every</u>   <u>only</u>
<u>other</u>   popu<u>lation</u>   <u>visitor</u>   How <u>often</u> ...?

- (Circle) two words with the sound .

- **Student's Book** Learn ♫ *Have, Go, Get* B p.141.

> The customer is always right.
> H. Gordon Selfridge

TRAVEL WITH ENGLISH 5

Words to learn

menu   starter   main course   dessert
order (*n.*, *v.*)   including   service   garlic
omelette   seafood   soup   strawberry   now

- Circle two words with the sound .

- Student's Book Learn 📖 Travel phrasebook 5 p.130.

■ Phrases

1 Match the situations and phrases.

1 You've got a cigarette but you haven't got any matches. — `e`
2 You're at a hotel reception desk. ☐
3 You're with a friend in a café. You're hungry. ☐
4 You're in your car at a petrol station. ☐
5 You're in a chemist's and you don't feel very well. ☐
6 You're at a post office with some postcards in your hand. ☐

a I'd like thirty litres, please.
b Have you got any aspirins, please?
c How much is a double room for two nights?
d I'd like five stamps for Canada, please.
e Have you got a light?
f Two coffees and a piece of cake, please.

■ Conversation

2 Complete the dialogue.

WAITER Good evening.
MAN Good evening. A ¹ *table* for one, please.
WAITER Come this way, please.

WAITER ² _____ you ready to order now?
MAN Yes. I'd like a tomato salad and then fish and chips, please.
WAITER Fine. What would you like to ³ _____?
MAN I'd ⁴ _____ a glass of white wine.

WAITER Would you like ⁵ _____ else?
MAN Yes, I'd like chocolate ice-cream and a black ⁶ _____ , please.

MAN Could ⁷ _____ have the bill, please?
WAITER Here you are, sir.
MAN ⁸ _____ me, I think the bill is wrong. Look, I had fish and chips, not steak and chips.
WAITER I'm very sorry, sir.
MAN That's OK. ⁹ _____ I pay by credit card?
WAITER I'm ¹⁰ _____ , sir. We don't take credit cards here.

■ Reading

3 a Read and complete the chart for the UK, Japan, and the USA.

Tipping around the world

In the UK, people usually leave a 10% tip for service in restaurants and cafés, at the hairdresser's, and in taxis. But they don't usually tip barmen in a pub. In Japan, people never leave a tip. And in the USA, the tip is usually 15% for everybody, including barmen.

	restaurants	cafés	hairdressers'	taxis	bars/pubs
the UK	10%				
Japan					
the USA			15%		
your country					

b Complete the chart for your country.

27

6 A

THE WIZARD OF ID — Brant parker and Johnny hart

Max's Story

'I love Martina, but ¹ she doesn't love ² me. Martina loves Hans. ³ He's very good-looking. I'm not good-looking, but ⁴ I'm quite rich. I've got a sister. ⁵ Her name's Louisa. ⁶ She likes Hans. Hans is lucky because two women like ⁷ him. But ⁸ he doesn't like ⁹ them. Hans only likes his parrot, Tonic. It's true, he loves ¹⁰ it!'

Tonic Max Hans Louisa Martina

Object pronouns

1 **a** Read Max's story. Write the names.

1 *Martina*   6 _____
2 _____   7 _____
3 _____   8 _____
4 _____   9 _____
5 _____   10 _____

b Complete.

1 *What* does Martina think of Max? *She doesn't love him.*
2 What does Max *think of* Martina? He _____ _____.
3 What _____ Hans think of Martina and Louisa? He _____ _____.
4 Why's Hans lucky? _____ two women like _____.
5 What does Hans think _____ his parrot? He _____.

Verbs + prepositions + pronouns

2 Write the sentences.

1 to listen her   *Listen to her.*
2 at look it   L_____
3 talk to him   T_____
4 you like do them?   D_____
5 help can you us?   C_____
6 for wait please me P_____

Adjectives

3 **a** Complete with positive or negative adjectives.

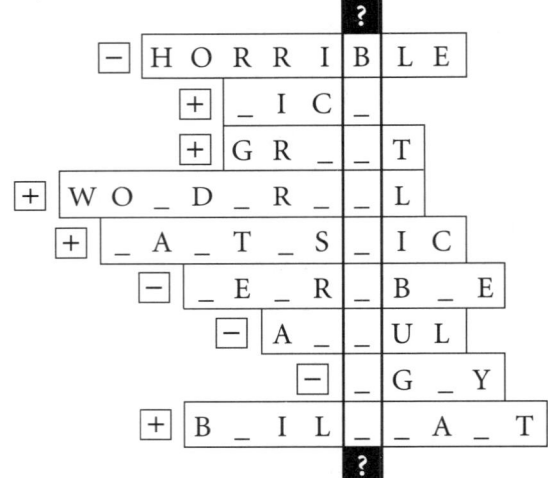

– H O R R I B L E
+ _ I C _
+ G R _ _ T
+ W O _ D _ R _ _ L
+ _ A _ T _ S _ I C
– _ E _ R _ B _ E
– _ A _ _ U L
– _ G _ Y
+ B _ I L _ _ A _ T

b What's the mystery adjective?

Words to learn

blues <u>country</u> and <u>western</u> pop mu<u>s</u>ician
<u>bo</u>ring her him it me them us you
Why not? be<u>cause</u>

- Circle three words with the sound [uː].
- Learn the adjectives in exercise 3.

28

Home, home, sweet, sweet home! There's no place like home!
John Howard Payne

6 B

■ Rooms

1 Which room is it?

1 There's usually a car here. *The garage.*
2 You sleep here. _____
3 You can cook in this room. _____
4 This is where you can wash or have a shower. _____
5 There are a lot of chairs and a table in this room. _____
6 This is where you can watch TV and relax. _____

■ *There is / are*

2 **a** Look at pictures A and B. Circle seven differences.

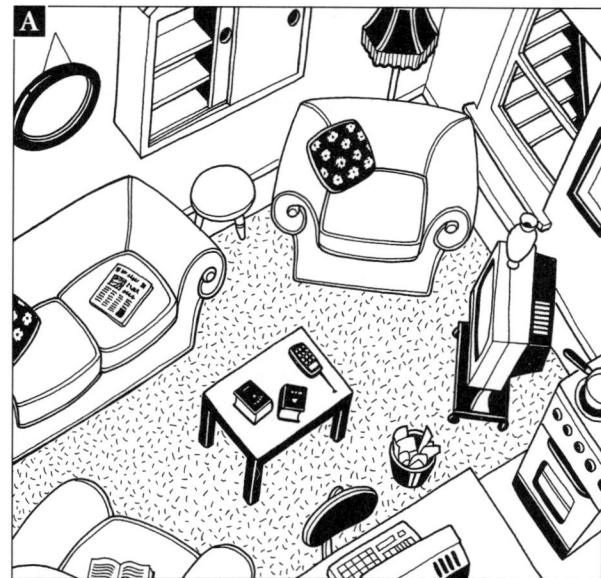

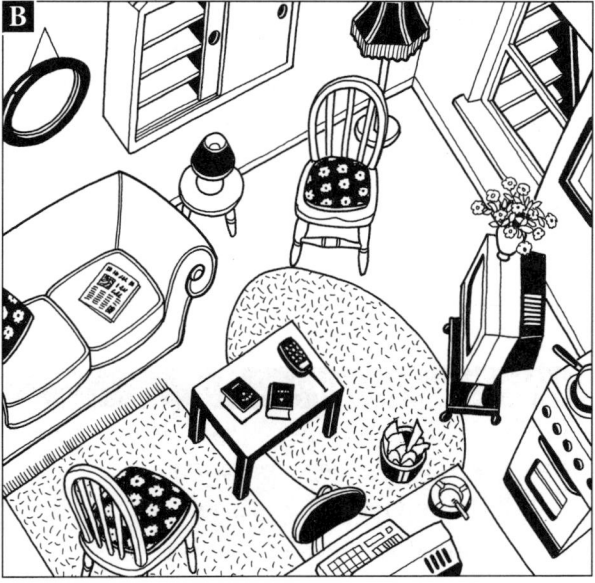

b Complete with *there's, there isn't, there are,* or *there aren't.*

1 *There are* four shelves in the cupboard in B but _____ only three shelves in A.
2 _____ any armchairs in B.
3 _____ one lamp in A but _____ two lamps in B.
4 _____ an ashtray in A.
5 _____ only five stairs in B but _____ six in A.
6 _____ some flowers in the vase in B but _____ any flowers in A.
7 _____ a carpet on the floor in A but _____ two rugs in B.

■ *a / some / any*

3 **a** Complete with *a* or *any.*

1 Are there are *any* shops in your street?
   Your answer _____
2 Is there ____ hospital in your town?
   Your answer _____
3 Are there ____ nice beaches near your town?
   Your answer _____
4 Is there ____ post office near your flat?
   Your answer _____

b Write your answers: *Yes, there is. / No, there isn't.* or *Yes, there are. / No, there aren't.*

c Complete with *some* or *any.*

1 There are *some* big hotels in my town.
2 There aren't ____ cinemas near my house.
3 There aren't ____ phone boxes in my street.
4 There are ____ mountains near my town.

Words to learn

<u>ash</u>tray <u>coffee</u> <u>table</u> <u>cush</u>ion plant stool
light-blue dark blue <u>love</u>ly <u>mod</u>ern

• Circle two words with the sound ∫ .

• **Student's Book** Learn ♪ **House** *p.138* and revise ♪ **Prepositions** *p.140*.

6 C

> No one called me pretty when I was a little girl.
> *Marilyn Monroe*

Thai Tours

Six-day tour of Thailand

Floating market

Pattaya Beach

Sunday: Arrive Bangkok airport. Flight to Chiang Mai.
Monday: Tour of Chiang Mai and elephant ride in the jungle.
Tuesday: Return flight to Bangkok.
Wednesday: Tour of Bangkok.
Thursday: Day-trip by bus to Pattaya, Thailand's best beach.
Friday: Visit Bangkok's floating market and Royal Palace.
Saturday: Return flight from Bangkok.

■ Reading

1 Read the tour programme. Answer the questions.

 1 Where do they sleep on the first night?
    _____

 2 How many different flights do they take?
    _____

 3 How many nights do they spend in Bangkok? _____

■ was / wasn't / were / weren't

2 Sandra was in Thailand with Thai Tours last week. Complete the dialogue.

MOTHER	So, darling. How ¹ *was* your holiday? ² _____ it exciting?
SANDRA	Yes. It ³ _____ . It ⁴ _____ great. Last Monday, I ⁵ _____ in the jungle – on an elephant!
MOTHER	Wow! And where ⁶ _____ you on Tuesday?
SANDRA	I ⁷ _____ in Bangkok.
MOTHER	⁸ _____ you with Terry?
SANDRA	No, I ⁹ _____ . He was in Pattaya, on the beach.
MOTHER	What about Sharon and Nick? ¹⁰ _____ they with you?
SANDRA	No, they ¹¹ _____ . They ¹² _____ in Pattaya with Terry.
MOTHER	So you ¹³ _____ alone?
SANDRA	Um, not exactly …

3 Complete the questions. Write the answers.

 1 *Was* Sandra in Bangkok on Tuesday?
    Yes, she was.

 2 _____ Sharon and Nick in Pattaya?
    _____

 3 _____ Terry in Pattaya?
    _____

 4 _____ Sharon and Nick in Bangkok?
    _____

 5 _____ Sandra alone in Bangkok?
    _____

■ at / in

4 Write the nouns in the right group.

~~bed~~   ~~the beach~~   France   home
the living-room   the sea   school   work

Yesterday afternoon, I was …

at	**in**
the beach	*bed*
_____	_____
_____	_____
_____	_____

Words to learn

murder body garage alone silent sure
upstairs   last *Monday* yesterday

- Which word is a verb *and* a noun?
- **Student's Book** Revise 📖 **Places** *p.133*.

> There never was a good war or a bad peace.
> Benjamin Franklin

6 D

The History Quiz

was / were

1 Tick ✓ true or ✗ false.

1. Julius Caesar wasn't the first Roman Emperor. ☐
2. There weren't any radios in the nineteenth century. ☐
3. The Vikings were from Norway. ☐
4. Pablo Picasso wasn't Spanish. ☐
5. There was a wall between East and West Berlin in 1990. ☐

Total ____ / 5

2 Complete and answer.

1. When *were* there dinosaurs on earth?
   a 300 million years ago b 10 million years ago
   c 100 million years ago
2. The Olympic Games _____ in Barcelona in
   a 1996. b 1992. c 1988.
3. What _____ Queen Victoria's husband's name?
   a Prince George b Prince Charles
   c Prince Albert
4. How many countries _____ there in the European Community in 1985?
   a nine b eleven c twelve
5. Who _____ the composer of *The Marriage of Figaro* ?
   a Mozart b Beethoven c Tchaikovsky

Total ____ / 5

There was(n't) / There were(n't)

3 Make true sentences.

1. There *weren't* any cars in the eighteenth century.
2. There _____ a revolution in France in 1789.
3. There _____ two world wars in the first half of the twentieth century.
4. There _____ a country called the USSR after 1991.
5. There _____ any women in *The Beatles* pop group.
6. There _____ two men on the moon in 1969.

Total ____ / 5

Total ____ / 15

■ Revision

4 Do the crossword.

Clues across →
1 British people drink in places called _____ . (4)
5 The opposite of *cold*. (3)
6 You can wash here. (8)
7 The Mediterranean is one. (3)
9 Don't _____ late tomorrow! (2)
10 He doesn't feel well, he feels *ill*. (3)
11 There are twenty in our classroom. (5)
12 Marilyn Monroe's real _____ was Norma Jean Baker. (4)
13 In the USA children start _____ at a quarter to nine. (6)

Clues down ↓
1 Artists paint _____ . (8)
2 We find 9 down in these. (8)
3 Darling! Your dinner's on the _____ . (5)
4 There were _____ papers on the floor. (4)
5 Doctors work here. (8)
8 I'm clever. I know _____ the answers! (3)
9 Most people sleep in them. (4)
12 The opposite of *yes*. (2)

Words to learn

back clue glass gun hand knife (*pl.* knives)
m<u>u</u>rderer un<u>u</u>sual

- Circle five words with the sound  .

- Student's Book Revise ✎ *Small objects* p.134.

6 TRAVEL WITH ENGLISH

It's never too late to learn.
English proverb

Focus on New Zealand

New Zealand is a country in the South Pacific, about 1,500 kilometres south east of Australia. It has two main islands: North Island and South Island. The capital city is Wellington in the centre of the country but the main city is Auckland in the north. It was part of the British Empire in the nineteenth century but it is now an independent state. There are about 3.5 million people and 66.5 million sheep. That's about twenty sheep for each person!

Country	❺ _____
Area	268,046 sq. km.
Capital	❻ _____
Population	❼ _____

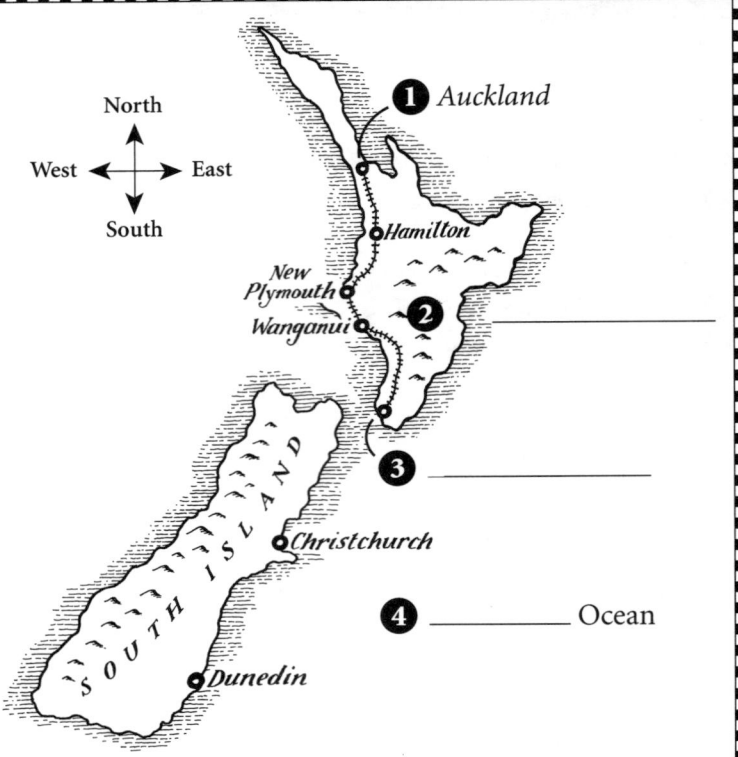

■ Reading

1 Read and complete the information on the map (1 to 7).

New Zealand Black Tour Special Rail Service				
Auckland	Hamilton	Wanganui	Wellington	
0730	0820	1045	1215	B
1220	1310	1535	1730	B
1700	–	–	2110	NS B

Key   NS No smoking train   B buffet car

Auckland – Wellington   single $110
                        return $185

2 Write the answers.

1 What time does the first train to Wellington leave Auckland? *0730*

2 What time does the last train to Wellington arrive? _____

3 How much is a return ticket to Wellington? _____

4 Is there a buffet car on all trains? _____

5 Can you smoke on the 1220 train to Wellington? _____

■ Revision

3 Match the phrases and answers.

1 I'm sorry. | d |
2 You're American. | |
3 Thanks a lot. | |
4 How are you? | |
5 Good luck. | |
6 Have you got a light? | |

a Thanks very much. The same to you.
b You're welcome.
c I'm sorry. I don't smoke.
d That's OK.
e Yes, that's right.
f Fine, thanks. And you?

Words to learn

leave   <u>arrive</u>   note (*n.*)   price   a bit
What ab<u>ou</u>t …?

Let's see.

- (Circle) two words with the sound  .

- **Student's Book** Learn 🧳 **Travel phrasebook 6** p.131 and revise **Classroom language** at the back of the book.

32

> But more, much more than this, I did it my way.
> *Frank Sinatra*

7 A

■ Present to past: *have / go / get*

1 Write the sentences in the past. Use the time expressions.

Present simple	Past simple
1 We get up early on Mondays. (last Monday)	*We got up early last Monday.*
2 He doesn't get to work late. (this morning)	He _____ get to work late this morning.
3 Does he have lunch every day? (yesterday)	_____
4 She has a bath at night. (last night)	_____
5 I go shopping at weekends. (last weekend)	_____
6 We don't go out a lot. (last Saturday)	_____
7 Does she go away on Fridays? (last Friday)	_____

■ Past tense: *be / have / go*

2 a Barry's on holiday in New York. Read his postcard and number the photos in order, 1 to 3.

b Complete the postcard. Use *had, went, was,* or *were*.

Dear Mum and Dad,
    This is a great holiday. Every day we do something different. We ¹ had a fantastic day yesterday! We ² _____ to Manhattan. It ³ _____ brilliant! We ⁴ _____ breakfast at the top of the Empire State Building – but we didn't see King Kong!
    Then we ⁵ _____ to Wall Street. At lunchtime we ⁶ _____ a picnic in Central Park. There ⁷ _____ hundreds of people there – all jogging! In the afternoon, we ⁸ _____ to the Museum of Modern Art. It ⁹ _____ wonderful. After that we ¹⁰ _____ to Chinatown. We ¹¹ _____ an enormous meal and it ¹² _____ really cheap.
    Hope you're both well. See you next Friday – if we come back!
        Lots of love
        Barry

■ Reading

3 Who is it? Use a dictionary.

Famous Europeans

A He was born in Corsica. He was a soldier. His wife's name was Josephine. He went to the island of St Helena in 1815. He didn't go back to France again. His initials are NB.

_____

B She was a beautiful Swedish actress. She went to Hollywood. She was the star of *Anna Karenina* and *Ninotchka*. She didn't make any films after 1941. Her initials are GG.

_____

C His father was the king of Macedonia in Greece. He was a great soldier. He had many battles with the Persians and Egyptians. He died when he was only thirty-two, in the year 323 BC. His name begins with the letter A.

_____

Words to learn

<u>f</u>ollow   stop <u>s</u>moking   ca<u>f</u>é   gym   de<u>te</u>ctive   <u>h</u>airdresser's

- (Circle) three words with the sound .
- **Student's Book** Learn 🔊 *Have, Go, Get* p.141 in the past tense.

7 B

> I came, I saw, I conquered.
> *Julius Caesar*

Past tense questions

1 Complete the dialogue.

1 A *Did you stay* in last night?
B No, I didn't. I went out.

2 A Where _____?
B I went to the cinema.

3 A What film _____?
B *Aladdin*.

4 A Who _____ with?
B With some friends and their children.

5 A What _____ after that?
B We went home.

Regular and irregular past tense verbs

2 Complete with the verbs in the past tense.

1 Hilary *bought* an expensive new stereo on Friday. (buy)
2 I _____ an interesting book last night. (read)
3 Marconi _____ the radio in 1902. (invent)
4 When I was at school I _____ Latin. (study)
5 We _____ cards for eight hours yesterday. (play)
6 They _____ that new French film last Sunday. (see)

Words to learn

buy   cook *a meal*   stay in   <u>study</u> *for an <u>exam</u>*
talk   <u>curr</u>y   mis<u>take</u>   b<u>u</u>sy

- Circle the word with the sound .
- List and learn fifteen irregular verbs from this page.

Study tip

☞ Start a list of irregular verbs. When you find a new irregular verb, add it to your list.

Reading

3 **a** Read about Charles Lindbergh. How long was his journey? _____

b Find the past tense of these irregular verbs.

1 make *made*   5 do   _____
2 say   _____   6 can   _____
3 think _____   7 begin _____
4 leave _____   8 fly   _____

c Find one past tense regular verb in the text.

Modern heroes: Charles Lindbergh

Every day thousands of people fly in comfortable planes over the Atlantic Ocean. They work, eat, sleep, read, or watch films during their safe, seven-hour journey. One man made this possible. His name was Charles Augustus Lindbergh.

In the 1920s planes were new, they were weak, and they couldn't travel very far. A New York businessman offered $25,000 to anybody who could fly the 3,600 miles from America to Europe. People said it was impossible!

But on 20th May 1927 Lindbergh, a pilot for the US Mail, began his journey from New York. The weather was terrible. Lindbergh's plane, the *Spirit of St. Louis*, was only made of wood and fabric. It didn't have a radio or lights, it didn't have heating, and it had only one small engine.

After twenty-four hours people thought Lindbergh was lost. After thirty hours they were sure he was dead. Then, suddenly, thirty-three and a half hours after he left New York, his plane flew over the Eiffel Tower in Paris. He did it! ✈

When I was born I was so surprised I didn't talk for a year and a half.
Gracie Allen

■ Reading

1 Do the months quiz.

1	How many months are there? *Twelve.*
2	Which is the third month? _____
3	How many months finish with '-ber'? _____
4	Which month has only three letters? _____
5	Which month has 'l' as the last letter? _____
6	Which month doesn't always have the same number of days? _____

■ Pronunciation

2 Write the words in the right group.

~~father~~   ~~fifth~~   thousand   those   thanks   with   the   third

ð	θ
father	fifth
_____	_____
_____	_____
_____	_____

■ Dates

3 Complete the chart.

Date	We say	We write	Celebration
4/7	the fourth of July	4th July	US Independence Day
25/12			Christmas Day
14/2			St. Valentine's Day
1/1			New Year's Day
31/10			Halloween

Study tip

☛ **Practise your English outside class.**

1 Make a list of birthdays to remember in English.

> Mum: 12th January
> Georgie: 2nd February

2 Write your diary in English.

> 12.00 Lunch with Mr Marx
> 3.30   Doctor's

■ Past simple: short answers

4 Complete the dialogue with *did(n't)*, *was(n't)* or *were*.

1 *Were* you at home last Saturday? Yes, I *was*.
2 And *did* James go out? Yes, he _____ .
3 _____ he go bowling? No, he _____ .
4 _____ he go to the football match? Yes, he _____ .
5 _____ it good? No, it _____ .
6 _____ he come home late again? Yes, he _____ .
7 And _____ you angry? Yes, I _____ !

Words to learn

was / were born die <u>a</u>nswerphone cheque <u>bi</u>rthday <u>boa</u>rding card date rec<u>ei</u>pt <u>ti</u>cket each

• ⓒircle the word with the sound .

• **Student's Book Learn 📖 Time C** *p.136*.

7 D

> I wanted to be famous. I wanted everybody to love me.
> *Madonna*

■ Regular past tense verbs

1 Complete the past tense forms of the verbs.

/t/	/d/	/ɪd/
wash*ed*	arrive___	rent___
pack___	change___	land___
type___	call___	wait___

Words to learn

book (*v.*) call disappear land (*v.*) pack
rent type <u>sudd</u>enly

- Circle two words with the sound 🔊 .

- **Student's Book** Learn ✏ **Irregular verbs** *p.144.*

2 a Complete with the verb in the past tense.

die   ~~discover~~   end   marry   murder   walk

1 Christopher Columbus *discovered* America in *1492*.
2 Neil Armstrong _____ on the moon in _____.
3 Prince Charles _____ Lady Diana in _____.
4 James Dean _____ in a road accident in California in _____.
5 The Second World War _____ in _____.

b Complete each sentence with the right year.

~~1492~~   1945   1955   1969   1981

■ Reading: A true story

3 a Read and complete the map. Draw the lines and write *by boat, by car, by lorry,* or *by train*. Use a dictionary.

b Find the past tense of these verbs. Are they regular (R) or irregular (I)?

arrive	arrived	R	sleep	___	☐
miss	___	☐	wake up	___	☐
decide	___	☐	take	___	☐
put	___	☐	catch	___	☐

c Add the irregular verbs to your list.

A one-day trip that took a week!

One day last summer Mr and Mrs Thomas Elham went to France for the day and came home ONE WEEK LATER!

Things began well. They arrived in Boulogne in the morning and they went shopping in the town. After that they went for a walk but they didn't speak French so they didn't understand the street signs. They got lost and missed the boat back to England. So they decided to get a train to Paris and then travel from Paris to London. But they got the wrong train and the next morning they arrived in Luxembourg! The police in Luxembourg put them on the train back to Paris. Mr and Mrs Elham slept well on the train – too well – they woke up in Basle, Switzerland!

A lorry driver took them back to Paris and they went to the railway station again. 'Unfortunately,' said Mrs Elham, 'we didn't understand the signs and we caught a train to Bonn, in Germany.' Mr and Mrs Elham finally caught a train back to Paris and a friendly police officer drove them all the way to Boulogne where they caught the boat back to Dover. They were six days late!

Based on information in *That's Life* (Treasure Press)

TRAVEL WITH ENGLISH **7**

■ Reading

1 Read and complete the chart.

Focus on the Netherlands

The Netherlands is a country on the north coast of Europe between Germany and Belgium. It's got a population of 15,010,000. The capital city is Amsterdam but the government is based in The Hague. The first language is Dutch but most people speak or understand English.

The Times Atlas of the World

Country _____
Population _____
Capital _____
Languages _____ / _____

■ Directions

2 You're at Schiphol Airport. Follow the directions. Where do you go to? Start between Tobacco and Cosmetics each time.

1 Turn left. Go past the Post office and it's on the left. *Audio / Video*

2 Turn right. It's on the left, opposite the Drugstore and Food. _____

3 Turn left. Go straight on. Go past Films and turn right. It's next to the stairs. _____

4 Turn right. Go past Cameras and turn left. It's on the right, behind Books. _____

5 Turn left. Go past Gifts and turn left again. It's on your left between Flowers and Fashion. _____

Words to learn

art gallery gift shop library palace town hall

- (Circle) the silent 'r'.

- **Student's Book** Learn 📖 **Travel phrasebook 7** *p.131* and revise ✎ **Prepositions** *p.140*.

3 Alana Altdorf is at passport control. Complete the dialogue.

ALANA Excuse me. ¹*Could* you tell me the way to the coffee shop?

SECURITY Yes, of course. Turn ² _____ and go ³ _____ the film shop. Then ⁴ _____ left. The coffee shop is ⁵ _____ the bookshop.

ALANA I'm sorry. I ⁶ _____ understand. Could you ⁷ _____ that again more slowly, please?

SECURITY Sure. You ⁸ _____ right, then left. It's next to the ⁹ _____ .

ALANA OK. Thanks.

SECURITY ¹⁰ _____ welcome.

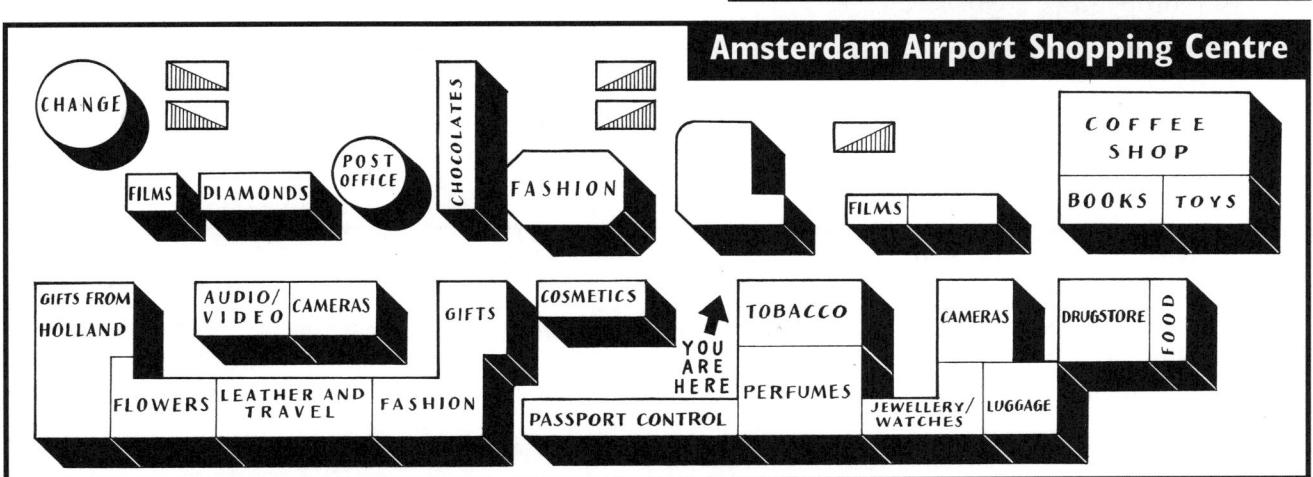

Amsterdam Airport Shopping Centre

8 A

> I'm singing in the rain, just singing in the rain.
> *Gene Kelly*

■ Present continuous

1 What are the guests doing? Complete with a verb.

call dance do look have play smoke sleep watch

1 The young couple *are dancing*.
2 The old man _____ a bath.
3 The young children _____ out the window.
4 The businessman _____ his wife.
5 The guest _____ TV.
6 The young woman _____ yoga.
7 The old woman _____ .
8 The teenagers _____ a video game.
9 The businesswoman _____ .

2 Write questions or negatives.

1 good any you reading books are [?]
  Are you reading any good books?
2 to isn't he the listening radio [−]
  _____
3 bags Cecilia why's her packing [?]
  _____
4 the aren't they at staying Ritz [−]
  _____
5 old are going where those men [?]
  _____
6 much isn't Rod studying very [−]
  _____
7 are at what you looking [?]
  _____

3 Match the lines from famous songs.

1 Raindrops are   [b]
2 All we are saying   [ ]
3 The answer is   [ ]
4 Falling in   [ ]
5 I'm dreaming   [ ]

a is give peace a chance *John Lennon*
b falling on my head *Sacha Diestel*
c of a white Christmas *Bing Crosby*
d blowing in the wind *Bob Dylan*
e love again, never wanted to *Marlene Dietrich*

■ Pronunciation

4 Write the words in the right group.

~~chicken~~ ~~evening~~ ~~garage~~ kitchen making much revision usually wrong

ʒ	tʃ	ŋ
garage	*chicken*	*evening*
_____	_____	_____
_____	_____	_____

Study tip

☞ Study English songs and titles. You can learn a lot of English from them. Write five titles that you know. Translate them.

Words to learn

happen neighbour photographer rain (*n.*)
a broken leg strange again probably

- (Circle) three words with the sound ŋ .
- **Student's Book** Revise 📖 *Verbs* p.139.

If you're going to San Francisco, be sure to wear some flowers in your hair.
Scott Mckenzie

8 B

■ Present continuous

1 **a** Match the sentences and people A to E.

1 Corinne's eating crisps. **E**
2 Simone's wearing glasses. ☐
3 Alex isn't wearing a jacket. ☐
4 Luisa and Tomas are dancing. ☐ ☐

b Complete and answer questions about the people.

1 *Is* Tomas having a good time? *Yes, he is.*
2 _____ Simone carrying a handbag? _____
3 _____ Luisa and Corinne wearing dresses? _____
4 _____ Alex and Corinne dancing? _____
5 _____ Simone enjoying the party? _____

■ Present simple / continuous

2 **a** Put the verb in the right tense.

1 Don't talk to Louis, he *'s doing* his homework. (do)
2 I _____ the paper every day. (read)
3 Clara's on the phone. She _____ to her husband. (talk)
4 His daughter _____ a dress today. (not wear)
5 'What do you do?' 'I _____ a doctor.' (be)
6 The children usually _____ their grandmother on Sundays. (visit)
7 'What are you doing?' 'I _____ for an exam.' (revise)

b Answer about you: *Yes, I am. / No, I'm not.* or *Yes, I do. / No, I don't.*

1 Are you wearing a T-shirt? _____
2 Are you wearing trousers? _____
3 Are you doing this exercise alone? _____
4 Do you usually study alone? _____
5 Are you sitting at a desk? _____
6 Do you often sit here? _____

■ Clothes

3 Write the words. Find the name of something you wear on your feet.

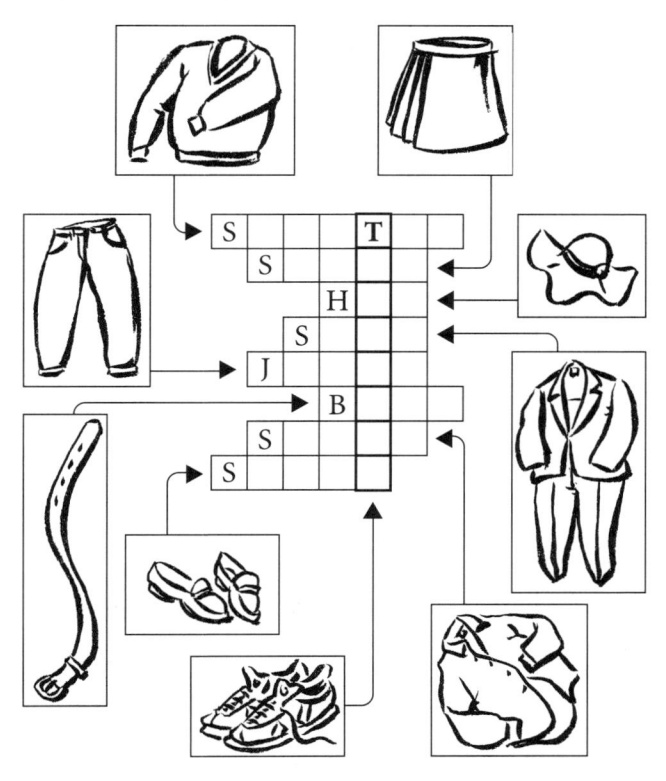

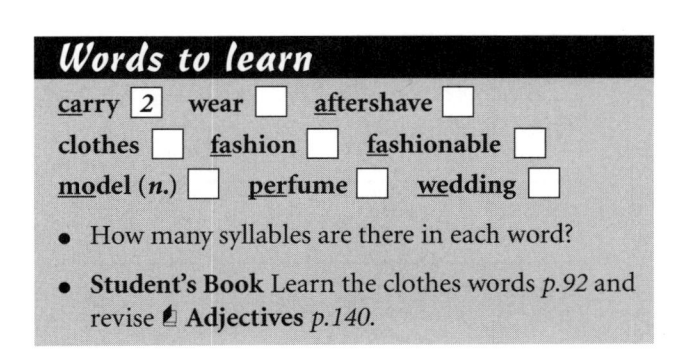

Words to learn

<u>car</u>ry ☐2 <u>wear</u> ☐ <u>aft</u>ershave ☐
<u>clothes</u> ☐ <u>fash</u>ion ☐ <u>fash</u>ionable ☐
<u>mo</u>del (*n.*) ☐ <u>per</u>fume ☐ <u>wed</u>ding ☐

- How many syllables are there in each word?
- **Student's Book** Learn the clothes words *p.92* and revise ⌂ **Adjectives** *p.140*.

8 C

> We're gonna rock around the clock tonight.
> *Bill Haley and the Comets*

(be) going to

1 a Look at pictures 1 to 5. What are their plans? Complete the questions and answers. Use contractions.

1. What's *he going to* do after work? *He's going to* have a sauna.
2. What _____ do tonight?
   _____ sleep.
3. Where _____ go this evening?
   _____ go shopping.
4. What _____ buy next year?
   _____ buy a motorbike.
5. How _____ spend the money?
   _____ travel round the world.

b Write negative sentences.

1. She / not / work
   She isn't going to work.
2. I / not / study
3. They / not / cook
4. We / not / go out
5. It / not / rain

2 Match the questions and answers.

1. Why are you turning on the TV? — c
2. Why are you studying?
3. Why are they buying rupees?
4. Why's Virginia packing?
5. Why's he cleaning his car?
6. Why are you closing the windows?

a Because they're going to travel around India.
b Because he's going to sell it.
c Because I'm going to watch the news.
d Because it's going to be cold tonight.
e Because she's going to spend the weekend in Oslo.
f Because we're going to do a test next Monday.

Tenses and time expressions

3 Write the time expressions in the right groups.

~~yesterday~~ tomorrow next week usually
in the 19th century next summer last year
on Tuesdays often

We usually use these words with the:

Past	Present simple	*be going to*
yesterday	_____	_____
_____	_____	_____
_____	_____	_____

Words to learn

<u>a</u>gree plan re<u>tire</u> win congratu<u>la</u>tions
fan<u>tas</u>tic next <u>week</u>end <u>spec</u>ial to<u>mor</u>row
to<u>night</u>

- (Circle) the irregular verb.
- **Student's Book** Revise ✎ **Irregular verbs** p.144.

> When the phone didn't ring I knew it was you.
> Roger McGough

TRAVEL WITH ENGLISH

8

■ Conversation

1 Match the sentence halves.

1 I'm sorry. I think [d]
2 Can I [ ]
3 I'll call [ ]
4 It's [ ]
5 Is [ ]
6 Just a [ ]
7 Hi. This [ ]
8 Please leave [ ]

a is Kim speaking. Can I help you?
b moment, please.
c a message after the 'beep'.
d you've got the wrong number.
e speak to Martha, please?
f that Ken Bradley?
g engaged.
h back later.

2 [a] Look at the pictures and dialogue opposite. Who's speaking? Complete the boxes with Mat (M), secretary (S), or receptionist (R).

[b] Complete the dialogue with the words.

| I'd like to | Hold | there | do | engaged |
| Could I speak | that | It's | ~~How can I~~ |
| One moment |

■ Reading

3 Match the words and definitions. Use a dictionary.

1 Freephone number [d]
2 Telephone chargecard [ ]
3 Fax machine [ ]
4 International code [ ]
5 Callbox / Payphone [ ]
6 Mobile phone [ ]

a You can use this phone anywhere.
b You can make a phone call here if you've got some money.
c You dial this number first to phone another country.
d It doesn't cost anything to dial this number.
e You can use this card to make phone calls on some public telephones.
f This machine uses phone lines to send and receive messages by phone on paper.

Receptionist

Mat Hendriksen

Secretary

[R] Spielmann Securities. ¹ *How can I* help you?
[ ] Good morning. ² _____ to Clara Schreiber in the sales office, please?
[ ] Clara Schreiber? ³ _____ , sir … I'm sorry, her line's ⁴ _____ .
[ ] Oh, is her secretary ⁵ _____ ?
[ ] ⁶ _____ the line please. It's ringing for you.
[ ] Sales office.
[ ] Oh, hello. Is ⁷ _____ Clara Schreiber's secretary?
[ ] Speaking. What can I ⁸ _____ for you?
[ ] ⁹ _____ Mat Hendriksen. ¹⁰ _____ leave a message for Clara.

4 Complete **Contractions file B** *p. 87*.

Words to learn

hold (*v.*)   leave *a message*   engaged
important   still   round *the world*

• (Circle) four words with the sound 🐟.

• **Student's Book** Learn 📘 **Travel phrasebook 8** *p.131*.

9 A

> Imagination is more important than knowledge.
> *Albert Einstein*

Words to learn

<u>hea</u>vy   common   valuable   dangerous
enjoyable   useful   less   oil   petrol   other

- <u>Under</u>line the stress.
- **Student's Book** Revise 🏠 House *p.138*.

■ Comparatives

1 **a** Write the comparatives.

1	heavy	*heavier*
2	long	_____
3	ugly	_____
4	nice	_____
5	expensive	_____
6	bad	_____
7	weak	_____
8	comfortable	_____
9	slow	_____
10	dangerous	_____

b Match the opposites.

a	stronger	☐	f shorter	☐
b	cheaper	☐	g less comfortable	☐
c	lighter	*1*	h faster	☐
d	more horrible	☐	i more beautiful	☐
e	safer	☐	j better	☐

3 Use the information to make a comparative sentence.

1. Sven 1.89 m / Erik 1.85 m (tall)
   Sven's taller than Erik.

2. Germany 356,840 sq km / France 543,965 sq km (small)
   _____

3. a Rolex watch $6,000 / a Casio watch $3,500 (expensive)
   _____
   _____

4. yesterday 5° C / today 11° C (cold)
   _____

5. an Olympic gold medal / an Olympic silver medal (good)
   _____
   _____

6. Princess Stephanie born 1965 / Princess Caroline born 1957 (young)
   _____

2 Make six true sentences.

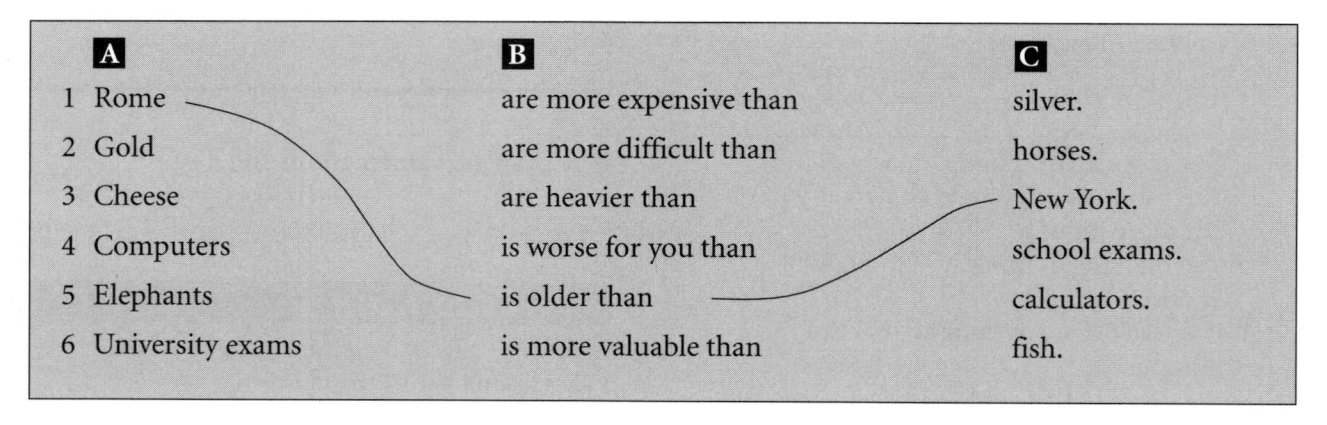

A	**B**	**C**
1 Rome	are more expensive than	silver.
2 Gold	are more difficult than	horses.
3 Cheese	are heavier than	New York.
4 Computers	is worse for you than	school exams.
5 Elephants	is older than	calculators.
6 University exams	is more valuable than	fish.

Everything's going to be all right.
Bob Marley

9 B

■ (*be*) *going to*

1 What are they going to do? Complete the sentences with the verbs.

have fall meet move ~~do~~

1 *They're going to do* an exam.
2 _____ on the floor.
3 _____ an accident.
4 _____ a stranger.
5 _____ house.

2 **a** Write the questions.

1 you / retire next year?
 A *Are you going to retire next year?*
 B I *don't* think so. I'm only fifty.

2 it / snow this weekend?
 A _____
 B I hope _____ . I love skiing.

3 the Social Democrats / win the election again?
 A _____
 B I _____ not. We need a new government.

4 Jane / meet us at the airport?
 A _____
 B I don't _____ so. She hasn't got a car.

5 they / get married this year?
 A _____
 B I think _____ . Maria bought a wedding dress last week.

6 Jack / study English in Britain next summer?
 A _____
 B M_____ . I'm not sure.

b Complete each answer with one word.

■ Reading

3 Read the text carefully. What's going to happen? Use the words in the list.

a baby   win   steal   the race   have
a lot of money

1 Mr Allenby's a bank manager. Yesterday he bought a one-way ticket to Buenos Aires. Now the bank's closed but Mr Allenby's got a key. He's carrying a large bag.
 He's _____

2 Alfred's running a marathon. He's an excellent runner. The race started two hours ago. He's in front. Now he can see the finish.
 He's _____

3 Janet got married five months ago. This morning she was ill. Now she feels very hungry. She wants to wear her jeans but they're too small. She's phoning her doctor.
 She's _____

Words to learn

have *an accident*   fall *in love*   move
meet *a stranger*   <u>ba</u>by   cloud   mara<u>th</u>on

I (don't) think so.   I hope so.   I hope not.
M<u>ay</u>be.

• (Circle) the word with the sound aʊ .

• **Student's Book** Revise ♦ *Have, Go, Get* p.141.

43

9 C

Time is a great teacher, but unfortunately it kills all its students.
Hector Berlioz

■ Adverbs

1 a Write the adverbs in the right group.

~~comfortable~~   ~~awful~~   happy   fast   slow
awful   easy   good   terrible

Spelling			
+ -ly	–e + -ly	–y + -ily	irregular
awfully	comfortably		

b Complete the second sentence with the adverb.

1 Pavarotti's got a beautiful voice.
   He sings *beautifully*.
2 She was a quick typist.
   She typed _____ .
3 They were bad drivers.
   They drove _____ .
4 Moira's a terrible tennis player.
   She played _____ .
5 He was very angry.
   He spoke _____ .
6 We're quite good dancers.
   We dance quite _____ .

■ Revision

2 Object pronouns Complete.

1 Where's Clarissa? I want to talk to *her*.
2 Who's that man? Why are you looking at _____?
3 *Schindler's List* was a good film. I liked _____ very much.
4 They've got a problem. Can you help _____?
5 We're going out tonight. Would you like to come with _____?

3 Prepositions Complete with the words.

about   at   by   for   from   in   of   on
~~to~~   until   with   to   for   in   to   at

1 We usually come *to* class _____ bus.
2 It always rains a lot _____ April.
3 Are they going to meet us _____ Sunday?
4 See you _____ the morning _____ 9.30.
5 He went _____ Thailand _____ Christmas.
6 She wasn't _____ home last night.
7 I lived in Mexico _____ 1989 _____ 1994.
8 Wait _____ me here _____ I come back.
9 I'd like a cup _____ tea _____ sugar, please.
10 Does he know much _____ computers?

4 Mixed tenses Match the questions and answers.

1 Do you live in London? [e]
2 Does your father live there? [ ]
3 Were you in the USA last year? [ ]
4 Did you go there with your sister? [ ]
5 Was the weather good? [ ]
6 Are you both going back next year? [ ]
7 Are you enjoying this interview? [ ]

a Yes, I was.
b Yes, I did.
c Yes. We hope so.
d Yes, he does.
e No, I don't.
f No, I'm not.
g Yes, it was.

Words to learn

smile   mine (*adj.*)   <u>qu**ie**tly</u>   <u>n**er**vously</u>
<u>sl**ow**ly</u>   Be <u>c**are**ful!</u>   Drive <u>c**are**fully!</u>

• (Circle) two words with the sound /eə/ .

• **Student's Book** Revise ♩ Time *p.136*.

> Life is like a tin of sardines – we're all looking for the key.
> Alan Bennett

9 D

■ Countable and uncountable nouns

1 Find sixteen food words. Write the words in the right column.

S	P	A	G	H	E	T	T	I
U	E	E	E	F	F	O	C	R
G	P	M	E	A	T	I	H	E
A	P	P	L	E	S	L	I	T
R	E	N	O	I	N	O	P	T
X	R	I	C	E	G	G	S	U
H	C	I	W	D	N	A	S	B
T	L	A	S	T	E	E	W	S
C	H	O	C	O	L	A	T	E

Uncountable	Countable
1 *spaghetti*	1 *onion*
2 _____	2 _____
3 _____	3 _____
4 _____	4 _____
5 _____	5 _____
6 _____	6 _____
7 _____	
8 _____	
9 _____	
10 _____	

■ a / an / some / any

2 Complete with *a*, *an*, *some*, or *any*.
1 I'd love *a* chocolate biscuit.
2 There isn't _____ sugar in the kitchen.
3 We're going to buy _____ fruit at the supermarket.
4 Would you like _____ egg for breakfast?
5 Did you buy _____ coffee?
6 My car's empty. I need _____ petrol.

■ How much? / How many?

3 Complete the questions and match the answers.
1 *How much* of a person is water? [c]
2 _____ states are there in the USA? ☐
3 _____ coke is there in a can? ☐
4 _____ kilometres are there in a mile? ☐
5 _____ sugar do you take in your tea? ☐

a About forty-five centilitres.
b Just a little, please.
c 60%.
d Fifty.
e About one and a half.

■ Puzzle

4 Write the missing word.
1 black / white   day / *night*
2 good / better   bad / _____
3 have / had   go / _____
4 train / station   plane / _____
5 hungry / hungrily   good / _____
6 shoes / feet   trousers / _____
7 jacket / clothes   sofa / _____

■ Pronunciation

5 Circle the word which rhymes.
1 *some* rhymes with *home* / (*come*)
2 *she* rhymes with *three* / *die*
3 *who* rhymes with *blue* / *know*
4 *these* rhymes with *this* / *please*
5 *live* (v.) rhymes with *five* / *give*
6 *where* rhymes with *hair* / *were*

Words to learn

need (to)   accountant   bottle   box   carton
packet   pasta   shopping list   tin

• Circle three words with the sound [ɒ].

• Student's Book Revise ♪ Food and drink p.135.

9 TRAVEL WITH ENGLISH

20% of American women think their feet are too big.

■ too + adjective

1 Write a sentence for each picture. Use words from the list.

expensive   long   ~~short~~   small

1 *They're too short.*
2 _____
3 _____
4 _____

■ Conversation

2 Match the questions and answers.

1 What size are you? [f]
2 Excuse me, have you got these in large? ☐
3 Can I help you? ☐
4 Excuse me, have you got this in grey? ☐
5 Can I try them on? ☐
6 Is this all right? ☐
7 Can I pay by credit card? ☐

a Of course. The changing rooms are on the left.
b No, thanks. I'm just looking.
c No, we haven't. But we've got it in black.
d Yes, madam. Visa or Mastercard?
e No, it's a bit too big.
f I'm not sure. Medium, I think.
g No, we've only got them in small and medium.

■ Revision: travel phrases

3 Where are they? Use the phrases.

clothes shop   hotel reception
fast food restaurant   Tourist Information
post office   restaurant   ~~street~~
Bureau de Change   phone   chemist's

1 Could you tell me the way to the bank?
  In the *street*.
2 Would you like a double room?
  At _____.
3 Excuse me. Can I try this on?
  In a _____.
4 I'd like a piece of pizza and a coke.
  In a _____.
5 Could I have ten stamps for Bulgaria?
  In a _____.
6 How much are these toothbrushes?
  In a _____.
7 Can I change $200, please?
  At a _____.
8 Could we have the bill, please?
  In a _____.
9 What time does the museum open?
  At _____.
10 I'll call back later.
   On the _____.

Words to learn

● **Student's Book** Learn 🧳 **Travel phrasebook 9** *p.131.*

46

My wife and I were happy for twenty years. Then we met.
Rodney Dangerfield

10 A/B

■ Revision crossword

Clues across →

1. What *does* he do? He's a taxi-driver. (4)
4. Do you live in a ___ or a flat? (5)
9. The old newspapers are in the bin, ___ the table. (5)
11. In the summer, I love going to the ___ . (5)
14. My father ___ to learn English for his job. (5)
15. Would you like tea ___ coffee? (2)
16. What time do you ___ get up? (7)
18. Do you think the party's going to be good? I hope ___ . (2)
19. Paul McCartney sings, 'I believe in ___ .' (9)
23. What do you think of ___ new car? We bought it last week. (3)
25. Another way to say *Hello*. (2)
26. When you learn a language, it's important to ___ a lot of questions. (3)
28. ___ they often work on Saturdays? I don't think so. (2)
29. The opposite of *stay in* is go ___ . (3)
31. Russia is ___ than Canada. (6)
33. We've got a problem. Can you help ___? (2)
34. The picture word for the symbol /ɪ/ is ___ . (4)
35. When I was on holiday, I ___ three detective stories. (4)
37. At Heathrow Airport, planes take off and ___ every minute. (4)
39. We ___ a terrible film at the cinema last Sunday. (3)
41. You go to this place to have a drink. (3)
42. At weddings, men usually wear a jacket and ___ . (3)
43. My grandmother always ___ in the afternoon after lunch. (6)
45. ___ cake would you like – this one or that one? (5)
47. Don't worry. Everything's going ___ be all right. (2)
49. Vegetarians don't ___ meat. (3)
50. This person wears a white uniform and looks after your teeth. (7)
53. David Bowie's got a blue one and a brown one. It rhymes with *my*. (3)
54. I'm very full. I think I ___ too much. (3)
55. I need to talk to you. Can you meet ___ after work? (2)
56. What colour are tomatoes? (3)
57. A lot of people do this to relax. (4)
58. The eleventh month. (8)

Clues down ↓

1. The opposite of *safe*. (9)
2. We go to the same club ___ Friday night. (5)
3. See you ___ Tuesday. (2)
4. 'What's ___ name?' 'Sophie.' (3)
5. He doesn't smoke ___ drink alcohol. (2)
6. We can't go out tonight because we're going to ___ for an exam. (5)
7. It's big and blue. People love to swim in it in the summer. (3)
8. '___ do you like Elvis Presley?' 'Because he had a great voice.' (3)
9. My sister ___ a computer at work. (4)
10. 'What did you ___ last night?' 'Nothing special.' (2)
11. London is famous for its big, red ___ . (5)
12. Another way to say *too*. (4)
13. It's a white or grey object and you see it in the sky. (5)
17. *Quickly, easily, fast,* and *well* are all ___ . (7)
20. An abbreviation: it means *for example*. (2)
21. *those / that, these / ___ .* (4)
22. Seventy-two, fifty-four, thirty-six, ___ . (8)
24. Another word for *street*. It rhymes with *showed*. (4)
26. She speaks English, German, ___ a little Russian. (3)
27. At the end of the *Happy birthday!* story, Clinton ___ Barney. (5)
30. A very big English-speaking country. (3)
31. My mother's going to retire on her sixty-fifth ___ . (8)
32. He was famous as Cary Grant but his ___ name was Archie Leach. (4)
36. Are they working at the moment? No, they ___ . (5)
38. We're going to Oslo ___ Wednesday. (4)
40. After the plane landed, Terri ___ for six hours. (6)
44. I'm hungry. I'd love a big ___ of chocolate cake. (5)
45. Are you going to ___ your new shoes tonight? (4)
46. I ___ going shopping at weekends. There are always too many people. (4)
48. 'Where are our coats?' 'They're ___ there, in the corner of the room.' (4)
51. A very British drink. It rhymes with *see* and *be*. (3)
52. They've got two daughters and a ___ . (3)
55. I left a message on his answerphone, but he didn't call ___ . (2)

10 C

> This is not the end. It is not even the beginning of the end.
> But it is, perhaps, the end of the beginning.
> *Winston Churchill*

■ Past simple and past participles

1 Complete the chart.

Regular verbs

infinitive	past simple	past participle
1 live	lived	lived
2 _____	stayed	_____
3 _____	_____	tried
4 watch	_____	_____

Irregular verbs

infinitive	past simple	past participle
5 be	was / were	_____
6 _____	_____	done
7 _____	had	_____
8 _____	_____	forgotten
9 _____	made	_____
10 meet	_____	_____
11 _____	saw	_____
12 take	_____	_____

■ Present perfect or past simple

2 Write sentences. Use contractions.
1. She never (try) Japanese food.
   She's never tried Japanese food.
2. He (not be) to the USA.
   He hasn't been to the USA.
3. They (live) in Germany and France.
   _____
4. you ever (meet) my sister?
   _____
5. I (have) three holidays this year.
   _____
6. We (not see) the film *Aladdin*.
   _____
7. Silvia ever (make) a pizza?
   _____

Words to learn

- Learn the past participles from exercise 1.
- **Student's Book** Revise 📖 *Irregular verbs* p.144.

---

3 **a** Alice is doing a survey. Complete her questions and the answers.

FLYAWAY TRAVEL Travel survey
Mr and Mrs Ross – Prague ✗   Miami ✓ last year
Leroy Blunt – Paris ✓ 1991   Caracas ✗

ALICE So, Mr and Mrs Ross. Have you ¹ *ever* been to Prague?

MRS ROSS No, we ² _____ .

ALICE Have you ever been ³ _____ Miami?

MR ROSS Yes, we ⁴ _____ . We went there ⁵ _____ .

ALICE Tell me, Leroy. Have you ever ⁶ _____ to Paris?

LEROY Yes, I ⁷ _____ . I went there in ⁸ _____ .

ALICE ⁹ _____ you ever been to Caracas?

LEROY No, I ¹⁰ _____ .

b Complete Alice's report about Leroy.

Mr and Mrs Ross haven't been to Prague but they've been to Miami. They went there last year.

Leroy Blunt hasn't _____
_____
_____

4 Translate and learn these phrases.
1. Have you ever been to Africa?
   _____
2. I've never been to South America.
   _____
3. I went to Australia last year.
   _____

48

Grammar check 1

Student's Book Look at **Grammar file 1** *p.17*

1 Verb *be*: contractions Complete the sentences.

	+			−	
1 I am	*I'm*	fine.	I'*m not* tired		
2 you are	_____	a student.	You	_____	a teacher.
3 he is	_____	Mexican.	He	_____	Brazilian.
4 she is	_____	from Vienna.	She	_____	from Salzburg.
5 it is	_____	a computer.	It	_____	a TV.
6 we are	_____	in room 10.	We	_____	in room 11.
7 they are	_____	African.	They	_____	European.

2 [a] **Questions / Short answers** Write the questions. Use capital letters. [b] Complete the answers.

	Questions		Answers
1 issheegyptian?	*Is she Egyptian?*		No, she *isn't*.
2 aretheyfromitaly?	_____		Yes, they _____ .
3 isthisyourpen?	_____		No, it _____ .
4 areyougerman?	_____		No, I _____ .
5 isitfridaytoday?	_____		Yes, it _____ .
6 areyoufromtokyo?	_____		No, we _____ .

3 Word order in questions Write questions. Use contractions.

1 your what is name ?   *What's your name?*
2 teacher is your who ?
   _____
3 York you are from New ?
   _____
4 today how you are ?
   _____
5 this his is file ?
   _____
6 they are from where ?
   _____

4 Imperatives Complete.

+	−
1 *Ask your teacher.*	Don't ask your teacher.
2 Listen to the cassette.	_____
3 _____	Don't look at your book.
4 Answer the question.	_____
5 _____	Don't write the words.

5 Possessive adjectives Complete with *my*, *your*, *his*, or *her*.

1 He's Chinese but _____ passport is American.
2 I'm from Milan and _____ name's Luigi.
3 What's _____ name? Where are you from?
4 She isn't here but _____ bag's on the desk.

6 Grammar words Match the word and example.

1 adjective	*d*	a What's her name?
2 capital letter	☐	b +
3 imperative	☐	c *be*
4 verb	☐	d tired
5 question	☐	e I'm not British.
6 negative sentence	☐	f Come here.
7 positive	☐	g A

Study tip

☛ **Compare English with your language.**

1 Look at **Grammar file 1** (**Student's Book** *p.17*). Learn the rules.
2 Is your language similar (S) or different (D)? Write S or D after each rule.

Grammar check 2

Student's Book Look at **Grammar file 2** *p.28*

1 **a** **Articles** Complete with *a* or *an*.
1 *an* airport
2 _____ dog
3 _____ egg
4 _____ hamburger
5 _____ snake
6 _____ year
7 _____ Italian film
8 _____ Chinese restaurant
9 _____ important phone number

b Complete with *a* / *an* or *the*.
1 Can I have *a* piece of paper, please?
2 Please look at *the* board.
3 They speak _____ little Japanese.
4 What does he do? He's _____ actor.
5 Have _____ nice day!
6 A is _____ first letter of _____ English alphabet.
7 What's this in English? It's _____ apple.
8 Where's _____ stress? Apple.

2 **Nouns** Write the plural.

Singular	Plural
1 a bus	buses
2 a language	_____
3 a computer	_____
4 a city	_____
5 a horse	_____
6 a sandwich	_____
7 a tree	_____
8 a monkey	_____
9 a bird	_____

3 **How much …? / How many …?** Complete.
1 *How much* is fifty pounds in US dollars?
2 _____ biscuits do you want?
3 _____ students are in your class?
4 _____ is a coffee and a large coke?

4 **this / that / these / those** Complete.

Singular	Plural
1 That's a fax.	*Those are faxes.*
2 _____ is good.	These pizzas are good.
3 Is this your key?	_____ your keys?
4 _____ jacket?	Do you like those jackets?
5 _____ free?	Are those seats free?
6 How old's that boy?	How old _____ ?

5 **Present simple** Write the negatives.

1 I work.	I *don't work.*
2 I know.	I _____ .
3 We like football.	We _____ .
4 They play tennis.	They _____ .
5 I speak Russian.	I _____ .
6 You understand.	You _____ .

6 **Questions / Short answers** Complete with *do* / *don't* or verb *be*.
1 *Do* you study French? No, I *don't*.
2 *Are* you married? No, we *aren't*.
3 _____ they work here? Yes, they _____ .
4 _____ your friends like Chinese food? No, they _____ .
5 _____ she South American? No, she _____ .
6 _____ he happy? Yes, he _____ .
7 _____ that your bag? No, it _____ .
8 _____ you want to learn English? Yes, I _____ .

7 **quite / (not) very** Write the sentences. Use contractions.
1 cold we quite are   *We're quite cold.*
2 they thirsty not are very   _____
3 very are hungry you ?   _____
4 hot it quite is   _____
5 is tired very he ?   _____

50

Grammar check 3

Student's Book Look at **Grammar file 3** *p.39*

1 Present simple: spelling Write the *he / she / it* form.

1 worry *worries*
2 go _____
3 say _____
4 dance _____
5 stop _____
6 use _____
7 have _____
8 be _____

2 a Questions / Short answers Read and underline twelve verbs.

Thomas Okoli from Nigeria

I live with my family in Lagos, Nigeria. I don't work. I study computer science. I want to be a computer programmer. In my free time, I meet my friends or watch TV. And I do a lot of sport. I play football and I run every day. I don't smoke and I don't drink alcohol.

b Complete. Use *does, doesn't, don't,* or *is*.

1 *Does* he live with his family? Yes, he _____ .
2 ____ he work? No, _____ .
3 ____ he a student? _____
4 ____ he study mathematics? _____
5 ____ he want to be a programmer? _____
_____
6 ____ he do a lot in his free time? _____
_____

c Write about Thomas. Change from *I* to *he*.
He lives with his family in Lagos, Nigeria. He …

3 Word order in questions Write the questions. Remember Q A S I.

That's my friend Marisa from Colombia.

1 Where / live? *Where does she live?*
  She lives in Bogota.
2 What / do? _____
  She's a travel agent.
3 What time / start work? _____
  _____
  She starts at 8.15 every morning.
4 What time / finish? _____
  _____
  She finishes at 7.30 in the evening.
5 What languages / speak? _____
  _____
  She speaks Spanish and a little English.
6 How old / be? _____
  She's twenty-six, I think.

4 can / can't Write the sentences.
1 swim can't we help *Help! We can't swim.*
2 I help can you sir ? _____
3 food can cook Chinese we _____
  _____
4 open window can please you the ? _____
  _____
5 have can coffee I a white please ? _____
  _____

The time

5 What's the time? Write the answers.

1 *It's a quarter past six.*
2 _____
3 _____
4 _____
5 _____

6 Complete the text.

¹ In India, the banks open ² ____ ten o'clock ³ ____ the morning. They close ⁴ ____ two p.m. five days a week and ⁵ ____ midday ⁶ ____ Saturdays. They don't open ⁷ ____ Sundays.

Grammar check 4

Student's Book | Look at **Grammar file 4** *p.50*

1 Adjectives Write sentences.
1. day (beautiful) — *It's a beautiful day.*
2. friends (old) — *They're old friends.*
3. flat (modern) — It _____ .
4. restaurant (expensive) _____
5. shoes (dirty) _____
6. town (famous) _____

2 Possessive adjectives Complete.
1. She lives with *her* brother and sister.
2. We live with _____ children.
3. Do you live with _____ family?
4. Do they live with _____ parents?
5. France is famous for _____ cheese.

3 a *have got* Write sentences. Use contractions.
1. he / video camera [+] *He's got a video camera.*
2. she / video [−] _____
3. they / fax [−] _____
4. we / new computer [+] _____
5. I / mountain bike [−] _____

b Write questions with *have got* and *a*, *an*, or *any*. Write the answer.

1. / he? ✓
   Has he got any cigarettes? Yes, he has.
2. / you? ✗
3. / she? ✓
4. / you? ✓
5. / he? ✗

4 Possessive 's Write sentences.
1. house (his friend) *It's his friend's house.*
2. husband (Julia)? Is he _____ ?
3. girlfriend (my brother)
   She's _____ .
4. cats (your aunt)?
   Are they _____ ?
5. children (the president)
   They're _____ .

5 *some / any* Complete.
1. They've got *some* new books to read.
2. We haven't got _____ clean cups.
3. I need _____ new shoes.
4. They've got _____ nice friends.
5. Has Greg got _____ brothers or sisters?
6. She knows _____ lovely places in Austria.

6 *like / love / hate* + (verb)-*ing* ✓ or ✗ ?
Correct the sentences.

I love	I like	I don't like	I hate

1. Lou likes shopping and driving.
   ✗ *He hates shopping.*
2. He loves eating in restaurants.
3. He doesn't like going to the cinema.
4. He doesn't like swimming.
5. He hates writing letters.
6. He likes cycling.

Grammar check 5

Student's Book | Look at **Grammar file 5** *p.63*

1 a Present simple: routines
Write about Colin Willis.

'I usually [get up] at [seven] and [have coffee] and [toast] for breakfast. After breakfast, I [have a shower] and then I go to work [by bus]. I get to work at [nine]. I work until [one] and then I [have lunch]. I start again at [two] and finish at [five]. I [do the shopping] before I go [home]. I get home at about [six forty-five]. I [have dinner] at about [seven thirty]. After dinner, I sometimes go out for a [drink] but I usually just stay at home and [watch TV]. I [go to bed] before [eleven]. My life isn't very exciting.'

He usually gets up at seven and has coffee and a piece of toast for breakfast. After ...

b
Look at Colin's answers. Write the questions. Remember Q A S I !

1 What / for breakfast? *What do you have for breakfast?* Coffee and toast.
2 When / shower? _____ After breakfast.
3 How / to work? _____ By bus.
4 What time / lunch? _____ At one o'clock.
5 What / after work? _____ I go shopping.
6 What time / home? _____ About six forty-five.

2 Articles
Complete with *the* or nothing (–).

1 She usually leaves __–__ home at eight.
2 Gabriel likes _____ cooking.
3 They work in _____ centre of Barcelona.
4 We usually have _____ breakfast together.
5 They often go to _____ bed early.
6 In July, I go to _____ beach every day.

3 Expressions of frequency
Write sentences.

1 often I forget names
   I often forget names.
2 come to doesn't class he usually
   He doesn't usually come to class.
3 Sergei exercise any never does
   _____
4 work day every does Tessa ?
   _____
5 once we play week golf a
   _____
6 birthdays always do you remember ?
   _____

4 have / have got
Change from *have* to *have got*. Use contractions.

1 We don't have | a mountain bike.
   We haven't got
2 He has | a microwave.
   _____
3 Do they have | a car? | Yes, they do.
   _____ | | Yes, they ____ .
4 He doesn't have any problems.
   _____
5 I have some American friends.
   _____

5 Prepositions of time
Write *in*, *on*, *at*, or nothing (–).

1 *in* the morning   7 ___ the weekend
2 ___ Tuesday   8 ___ Tuesday night
3 ___ 6.30   9 ___ dinner-time
4 ___ March   10 ___ midnight
5 ___ tonight   11 ___ this evening
6 ___ next lesson   12 ___ tomorrow night

Grammar check 6

Student's Book Look at **Grammar file 6** *p.72*

1 Pronouns Complete with object pronouns.
1 Bye! See *you* on Monday.
2 'Why do you drink black tea?'
   'Because I like _____!'
3 'What do you think of politicians?'
   'I hate _____.'
4 'We've got a problem. Can you help _____?'
   'Sorry, I'm busy now. Can you come and see _____ this afternoon?'
5 'Does Peter love Maria?'
   'Yes. He wants to marry _____ but she doesn't love _____.'

2 a *There is / are + a / some / any* Complete.

Singular	Plural
+ There's a TV.	*There are some* CDs.
− There isn't a chair.	_____ chairs.
? _____ sofa?	Are there any sofas?

b Write sentences.
1 / shelves behind / desk +
   There are some shelves behind the desk.
2 / radios in / window −
   _____
3 / plants on / shelves +
   _____
4 / people in / window ?
   _____

3 a Verb *be*: past simple Where were they yesterday? Write sentences.

1 *He was at work.*   4 _____ home.
2 _____ bed.   5 _____ garden.
3 _____ park.

b Complete with *was / wasn't* or *were / weren't*.
1 '*Was* it your birthday last week?'
   'Yes, it _____.'
2 '_____ you at home last Wednesday?'
   'No, I _____.'
3 'Where _____ your brother last month?'
   'He _____ in Lisbon.'
4 '_____ your parents at the party?'
   'No, they _____.'
5 'Where _____ you this morning?'
   'I _____ at the dentist's.'

4 *There was / were* Complete with the right form, +, −, or ?.
1 I'm sorry we're late. *There was* a lot of traffic.
2 '_____ _____ a football match on TV last night?' 'No, _____ _____.'
3 '_____ _____ a lot of guests at the wedding?' 'Yes, _____ _____ about three hundred people.'
4 '_____ _____ a photo of you in the paper yesterday!'
5 _____ _____ three letters for you this morning but _____ _____ any postcards.
6 _____ _____ many students in class last Friday. Only two!

Grammar check 7

Student's Book | Look at **Grammar file 7** *p.89*

1 Present to past Complete.

	Present	Past
+ a	We live in Jakarta.	We *lived* in Jakarta.
b	He lives in a flat.	He _____ in a flat.
− c	They don't need it.	They _____ need it.
d	She doesn't speak French.	She _____ speak French.
? e	_____ you have lunch?	_____ you have lunch?
f	What _____ she do?	What _____ she do?

Study tip

☛ **Compare tenses** Study the chart. Which has more forms? Present simple / Past simple.

2 Regular verbs: spelling Write the verbs in the past tense.

call *called*	close _____	love _____
stop _____	try _____	wash _____
work _____	worry _____	

3 Irregular verbs Complete.

Infinitive	Past tense	Negative
1 can	*could*	couldn't
2 get	_____	didn't get
3 _____	went	didn't _____
4 _____	_____	didn't have
5 leave	_____	didn't _____
6 _____	_____	didn't meet
7 _____	read	didn't _____
8 _____	_____	didn't say
9 see	_____	didn't _____
10 take	_____	didn't _____

4 Questions Complete the questions. Remember ⎕Q⎕ ⎕A⎕ ⎕S⎕ ⎕I⎕ !

1 Where *did* you *go*? Bali.
2 Who _____ with? I went alone.
3 Why _____ there? On business.
4 How _____ there? By plane.
5 How long _____? Four days.
6 Where _____? In a five-star hotel.
7 _____ any photos? Yes, I took a lot of photos.
8 _____ a good time? Yes, I had a great time!

5 Regular and irregular verbs Complete with the verbs in the past.

(not) be   cannot   drive   ~~see~~   get
(not) have   play   read   ~~stay~~   watch   look

1 We *stayed* at home last night but we didn't _____ television. We _____ some computer games.
2 I *saw* all *The Godfather* films and I _____ the book.
3 We _____ 30 km to a famous restaurant but we _____ a very good meal.
4 She _____ for her keys but she _____ find them.
5 He _____ a taxi. Luckily it _____ very expensive.

6 Past time expressions Match the sentence halves.

1 They worked in Sicily for [c]
2 She was born thirty years [ ]
3 We travelled to China in [ ]
4 They got a new car [ ]
5 Leonardo da Vinci was born on [ ]
6 I didn't do very much last [ ]
7 You spoke to her at [ ]

| a 1994.
| b April 15th, 1452.
| c fifteen years.
| d night.
| e yesterday.
| f half past eleven.
| g ago.

Grammar check 8

Student's Book Look at **Grammar file 8** *p.100*

1 Present continuous What are they doing? Complete the sentences and questions. Use the verbs.

~~check in~~ fly (x 2) talk (x 3) cry (x 2) cut

¹ *He's checking in* at the airport.
Where ² _____ to?
³ _____ to Hawaii.

⁴ _____ on the phone.
Who ⁵ _____ to?
⁶ _____ to her bank manager.

⁷ _____ .
Why ⁸ _____ ?
Because ⁹ _____ onions.

2 Present simple or present continuous? Choose the correct tense.

1 a Do you read
   b Are you reading | this exercise now?

2 a They don't watch
   b They aren't watching | TV very often.

3 a I don't look
   b I'm not looking | for a new job.

4 a What do you wear
   b What are you wearing | at work?

3 **a** *(be) going to …* Complete the sentences.

1 *I'm going to* run a marathon tomorrow. [+]
2 We _____ get a microwave. [−]
3 ___ you _____ retire soon? [?]
4 They _____ come next summer. [−]
5 ___ he _____ help you? [?]
6 She _____ do her homework tonight. [+]

b Write the questions. Use contractions.

1 they going when married to are get ?
   When are they going to get married?
2 is to what she the going wear wedding to ?
   _____
3 what you going give to are them ?
   _____
4 where to they going that go are after ?
   _____

4 Future time expressions Match the sentence halves.

1 Are you going to study at   [d]
2 He's going to South America next   [ ]
3 Are we going to the cinema   [ ]
4 She isn't going to meet us tomorrow   [ ]
5 They aren't going to work in   [ ]

a the summer.
b evening.
c month.
d the weekend?
e tonight?

5 *it* Complete with *it* + verb *be* (past or present).

1 A *Is it* raining?
   B No, _____ .
2 A _____ very hot last weekend.
   B Yes, but _____ going to be cold next week.
3 A What's the time?
   B _____ a quarter to seven.
   A Oh, no! _____ very late. Let's go.

56

Grammar check 9

Student's Book | Look at **Grammar file 9** *p.112*

1 **a** **Comparative adjectives** Write the comparatives in the right group.

bad   difficult   easy   ~~sad~~   good   hungry
important   near   ~~small~~   thin

+ -er	double consonant	-ier
smaller	sadder	_____
_____	_____	_____

more / less	irregular
_____	_____
_____	_____

b Write sentences.
1 Diamonds are *more valuable* than gold. (valuable)
2 My father's _____ than me. (fat)
3 London's _____ than New York. (old)
4 Milk's _____ than water. (expensive)
5 Water's _____ than ice. (heavy)
6 Arthur's _____ than her. (young)

2 **Predictions: (be) going to …** What's going to happen? Complete with the verbs.

be   have   ~~rob~~   see   win

1 He's *going to rob* the bank.
2 We'_____ _____ a film. 
3 She'_____ _____ the race. 
4 They'_____ _____ an accident. 
5 Oh, no! I'_____ _____ late. 

3 **Adverbs of manner** Change the sentence. Use the same adjective to make the adverb.
1 It was a really bad game.
   Both teams played really *badly*.
2 He's happy.   He's smiling _____ .
3 They were quick workers.
   They worked _____ .
4 Their English is very good.
   They speak English very _____ .

4 **Countable / Uncountable nouns** Write *C* or *U*.
1 cup [C]   4 hand [ ]   7 salt [ ]
2 petrol [ ]   5 hat [ ]   8 toothbrush [ ]
3 rain [ ]   6 man [ ]   9 money [ ]

5 *a / an / some / any* Complete.
1 We bought *some* nice fruit yesterday.
2 I haven't got _____ very good car.
3 There aren't _____ shops in our street.
4 Are there _____ tissues in that box?
5 I'd like _____ apple, please.
6 There was _____ cheese in the fridge but there weren't _____ eggs.
7 Would you like _____ more coffee?

6 *How much …? / How many …?* Complete the questions. Use the right tense.
1 He bought some fruit juice.
   How *much did he* buy?
2 She took a lot of photos.
   How _____ take?
3 I don't drink a lot of coffee.
   How _____ drink?
4 They spent a lot of money.
   How _____ spend?
5 I'd like some oranges.
   How _____ like?

57

Grammar check 10

Spelling patterns and tense revision

1 Irregular spelling patterns Look at the chart. Then do questions 1 to 6.

Words ending	Change	Grammar endings	Examples	
-ch -sh -s -ss -x -o	add -e	-s	watch finish bus address box potato	watches finishes buses addresses boxes potatoes
-e	✗	-ing	write dance	writing dancing
		-ed	like live	liked lived
-y	-y → -ie	-s	study country	studies countries
		-d	try marry	tried married
	-y → -i	-ly	easy angry	easily angrily
		-er	happy heavy	happier heavier
one consonant + one vowel + one consonant	double the consonant	-ing	shop run	shopping running
		-ed	plan stop	planned stopped
		-er	hot win	hotter winner

Key to grammar endings	
-s = present simple (*he / she / it*) and plural nouns -ing = present continuous and -ing nouns	-ed = past simple and past participles -ly = adverbs -er = comparative adjectives

1 Write the **plural**.
   sandwich*es* fax__ kiss__
   tomato__ family _____
   city _____

2 Write the **adverb**.
   heavy *heavily* lucky _____
   quick__ careful__
   happy _____

3 Write the **comparative**.
   big*ger* hot__ thin__
   funny _____ busy _____

4 Write the **past tense**.
   worry *worried* need__ prefer__
   smoke__ study _____

5 Write the **third person form**.
   wash*es* teach__ go__ do__
   wait__ try _____

6 Write the **-ing form**.
   make *making* drive _____
   come _____ swim__
   get__

2 Changing tenses Write the sentences in the past and future.

Present simple	Past simple	Future
1 I start at 9.00.	*I started at 9.00.*	*I'm going to start at 9.00.*
2 We watch TV.		
3 She works in a bank.		
4 I don't smoke.		
5 He doesn't play cards.		
6 Do they have breakfast?		
7 Does she drive to work?		
8 What does she do?		
9 Where do you study?		

Read and write

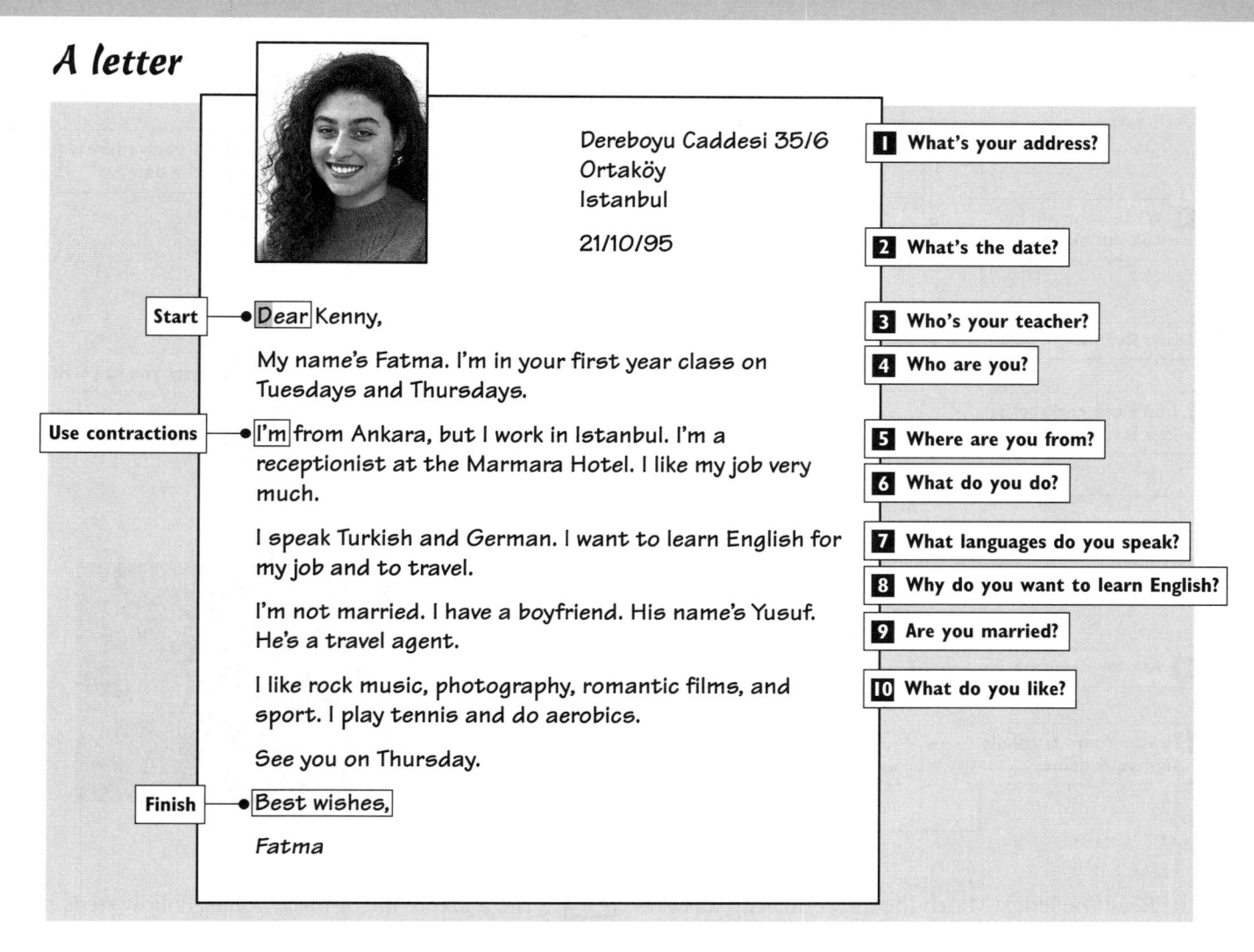

Files 1 and 2

A letter

Dereboyu Caddesi 35/6
Ortaköy
Istanbul

21/10/95

Start → Dear Kenny,

My name's Fatma. I'm in your first year class on Tuesdays and Thursdays.

Use contractions → I'm from Ankara, but I work in Istanbul. I'm a receptionist at the Marmara Hotel. I like my job very much.

I speak Turkish and German. I want to learn English for my job and to travel.

I'm not married. I have a boyfriend. His name's Yusuf. He's a travel agent.

I like rock music, photography, romantic films, and sport. I play tennis and do aerobics.

See you on Thursday.

Finish → Best wishes,

Fatma

1. What's your address?
2. What's the date?
3. Who's your teacher?
4. Who are you?
5. Where are you from?
6. What do you do?
7. What languages do you speak?
8. Why do you want to learn English?
9. Are you married?
10. What do you like?

1 Read the letter and complete the form.

```
Name        Fatma
Address
Nationality
Job
Languages   a little English,
Marital status
Likes
```

2 Correct the mistake.

1 Dear Mr Kenny,   *Dear Kenny,*
2 I from Ankara. _____
3 I'm receptionist. _____
4 I like very much my job. _____
_____
5 I speak turkish. _____
6 I want learn English. _____
7 I have boyfriend. _____
8 I like the rock music. _____

3 Study the letter. Use a marker pen to highlight.
a the capital letters (D)
b the full stops (.)
c the word *and*

✎ Write a similar letter to your teacher.

- Answer questions 1 to 10. Say more if you want to.
- Use a dictionary.
- Remember capital letters and full stops.
- Sign your first name.
- Read your letter. Check it carefully.
- Give it to the teacher.

New words

Dear   boyfriend   photography   romantic
Best wishes   letter   correct   mistake
marker pen   highlight   carefully

Read and write

File 3

A fax

1 Write: To: + the name
From: + your name.

2 Write the number of pages.

```
To: ROYAL CIRCUS HOTEL
From: Helena Stastny
Tel: 07 563 221
Fax: 07 343 518
```

1 page

Jesenskeho ul
   1992/27-4
Bratislava
8 5 1 73
SLOVAKIA
10.6.95

3 Write your address and the date.

4 Write your phone and fax number.

5 Start: Dear Sir / Madam,

Dear Sir / Madam,

I am writing to make a reservation.

I would like two double rooms with private bathrooms. We need one room with a double bed, and one with two single beds.

We would like to stay for four nights from 7.8.95 to 10.8.95.

I have two questions:
1 Does the hotel have a swimming pool?
2 Do you have a TV in every room?

Please write or fax to confirm.

Thank you very much for your help.

Yours faithfully,

Helena Stastny

6 Don't use contractions in a formal letter.

7 Say why you are writing.

8 Say what you want.

9 Ask for confirmation.

10 Finish: Yours faithfully, Sign your name.

The Royal Circus Hotel ★★★

---

1 Read the letter. Match the questions and answers.

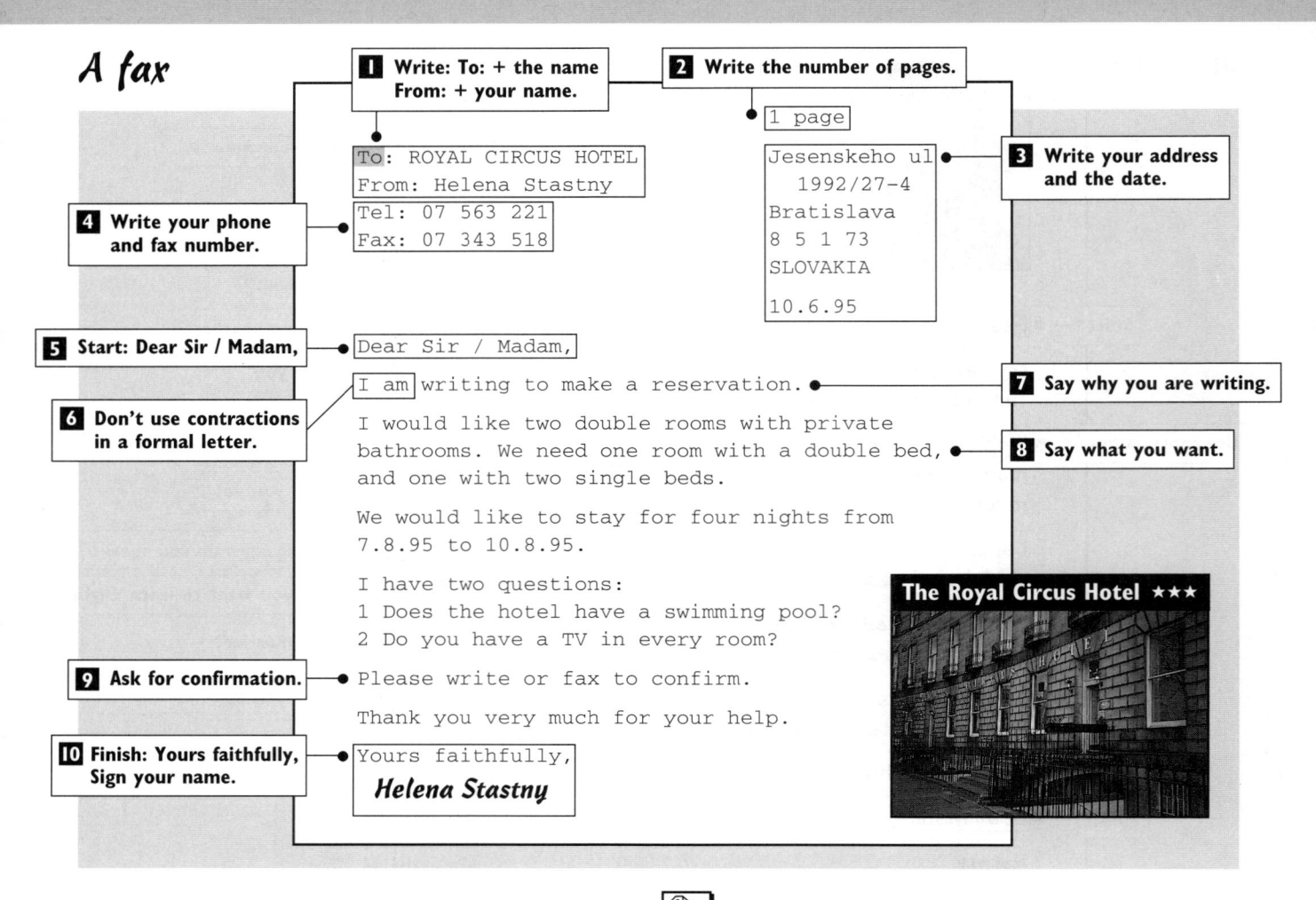

1 Who's the fax from? — *e*
2 Who's the fax to?
3 How many pages is the fax?
4 How many rooms would she like?
5 How many beds does she want?
6 How many nights would she like to stay?

a One.
b Two.
c Three.
d Four.
e Helena Stastny.
f The Royal Circus Hotel.

2 a Find and highlight these words in the fax.

to (x 5)   from (x 2)   for (x 2)   with (x 3)   in

b Complete the sentences.

1 We are writing *to* make a reservation.
2 I would like ___ stay ___ three nights.
3 Please phone or fax ___ confirm.
4 Thank you ___ your help.

✏️ Write a fax to one of these hotels. Follow steps 1 to 10.

Hotel Pariz Prague

Turtle Bay Hilton Hawaii

Sydney Boulevard Hotel Sydney

- Make a reservation for you and four friends for six nights in June.
- Ask two questions about the hotel. Use words in the list.

   a car park?   a sauna?   a restaurant?
   a café?   non-smoking rooms?

- Read your fax. Check it carefully.
- Give it to the teacher.

New words

I'm <u>writing</u> to …   <u>swimming</u> pool   every
con<u>firm</u>   confir<u>mation</u>   formal
Yours <u>faithfully</u>   sauna

60

Read and write

File 4

A description

A good friend

This is a photo of my friend Endang. She's from Indonesia.

She lives with her parents in Jakarta. They've got a new flat near the centre.

She's a nurse <u>and</u> she works at the hospital. She likes her job very much but it isn't easy. She speaks Bahasa, Indonesian, and a little English.

She likes swimming and cooking. She loves listening to pop music and dancing.

She's twenty-two years old. She's small and quite thin. She's got dark eyes and long black hair. I think she's got a lovely face.

- [ ] What does she do?
- [ ] How old is she?
- [1] Who is it?
- [ ] Where does she live?
- [ ] What does she do in her free time?
- [ ] Where's she from?
- [ ] Does she like her job?
- [9] Describe her.
- [ ] What languages does she speak?

A famous person

A He loves running <u>and</u> he does yoga. He's very healthy. He doesn't smoke or drink alcohol.

B He's about forty-six years old. He isn't very tall but he's quite attractive. He's got blue eyes and brown hair. He's got an interesting face and he's very funny.

C 1st This is a photo of Robin Williams. He's from Michigan in the USA.

D He lives in a large house near San Francisco with his second wife, Marsha. They've got two children, Zelda and Cody, and he's got one child, Zachary, from his first marriage.

E He's a comedian and actor. He's the voice of the genie in Disney's *Aladdin* and he's in *Good Morning Vietnam* and *Mrs Doubtfire*. He likes his job but he doesn't work all the time. He speaks English and French.

1. **a** Read about Endang. Number the questions from 1 to 9.

   b <u>Underline</u> the words *and* and *but*.

   c Highlight the ten adjectives.

2. **a** Now read about Robin Williams. Number the paragraphs 1st to 5th in the same order as Endang's description.

   b <u>Underline</u> the words *and* and *but*.

   c Highlight the twelve adjectives.

Find a picture of a friend or a famous person. Write a description in five paragraphs.

- Answer questions 1 to 9.
- Use *and* and *but*.
- Read and check it carefully.
- Give the picture and description to the teacher.

New words

<u>lovely</u> face <u>yoga</u> <u>healthy</u> <u>interesting</u> voice <u>genie</u> <u>marriage</u> <u>description</u>

Read and write

File 5

An article for a magazine

My favourite day is ...

This week we talk to Hisham Ali, a 28-year-old taxi-driver from Alexandria in Egypt. His favourite day is Friday. We also talk to Eva Mont, 52, a doctor from Viña del Mar in Chile.

Hisham works every day except Fridays.

'On Fridays, I usually get up quite early, have breakfast with my wife and children, read the paper, and maybe go for a walk.

Before lunch, I always go to the mosque. After that I spend the day with my family. We often have a picnic at the beach. After lunch, I relax and play with my children.

In the evenings, I usually watch TV or a video. We sometimes go to the cinema, or I go to a café and play backgammon with my friends.'

Eva lives alone in a flat near the beach.

'I love Sundays! I always have breakfast in bed. I get up late, at about ten o'clock. In the winter, I go skiing in the mountains. In the summer, I go for a run on the beach.

Then I have lunch, usually with friends. We sit in the sun, eat, talk, and relax. That's my favourite time. It's lovely.

On Sunday evenings, I always go to church. After that, I read or play cards. I hardly ever watch TV. I never go to bed before midnight.'

Remember to use connectors

B 1st

1 **a** Read about Hisham. Number photos A to C in the right order, 1st to 3rd.

   b Read about Eva. Number photos D to F 1st to 3rd.

2 Complete with *Hisham* or *Eva*.

   1 *Eva* does a lot of sport.
   2 _____ always goes to the mosque on Fridays.
   3 _____ sometimes goes out in the evenings.
   4 _____ usually gets up and goes to bed late.
   5 _____ spends the day with the family.
   6 _____ doesn't usually watch television.

3 Highlight six different adverbs of frequency.

Write an article for the magazine. Use the questions to help you. Write three paragraphs.

- What's your favourite day of the week? What do you usually do:
  1 **in the morning?**
     Do you get up early or late?
     Do you have a big breakfast?
     Do you do any sport?
  2 **in the afternoon?**
     Where do you have lunch? Who with?
     What do you do after that?
  3 **in the evening?**
     Do you go out or stay in?
     Do you go to bed late?
- When you finish read and check it carefully.
- *Don't* write your name on the paper. Give it to the teacher.

New words

mosque   picnic   **backgammon**
go for *a walk* / *run*   sun   *maga*zine article

Read and write

File 6

A composition

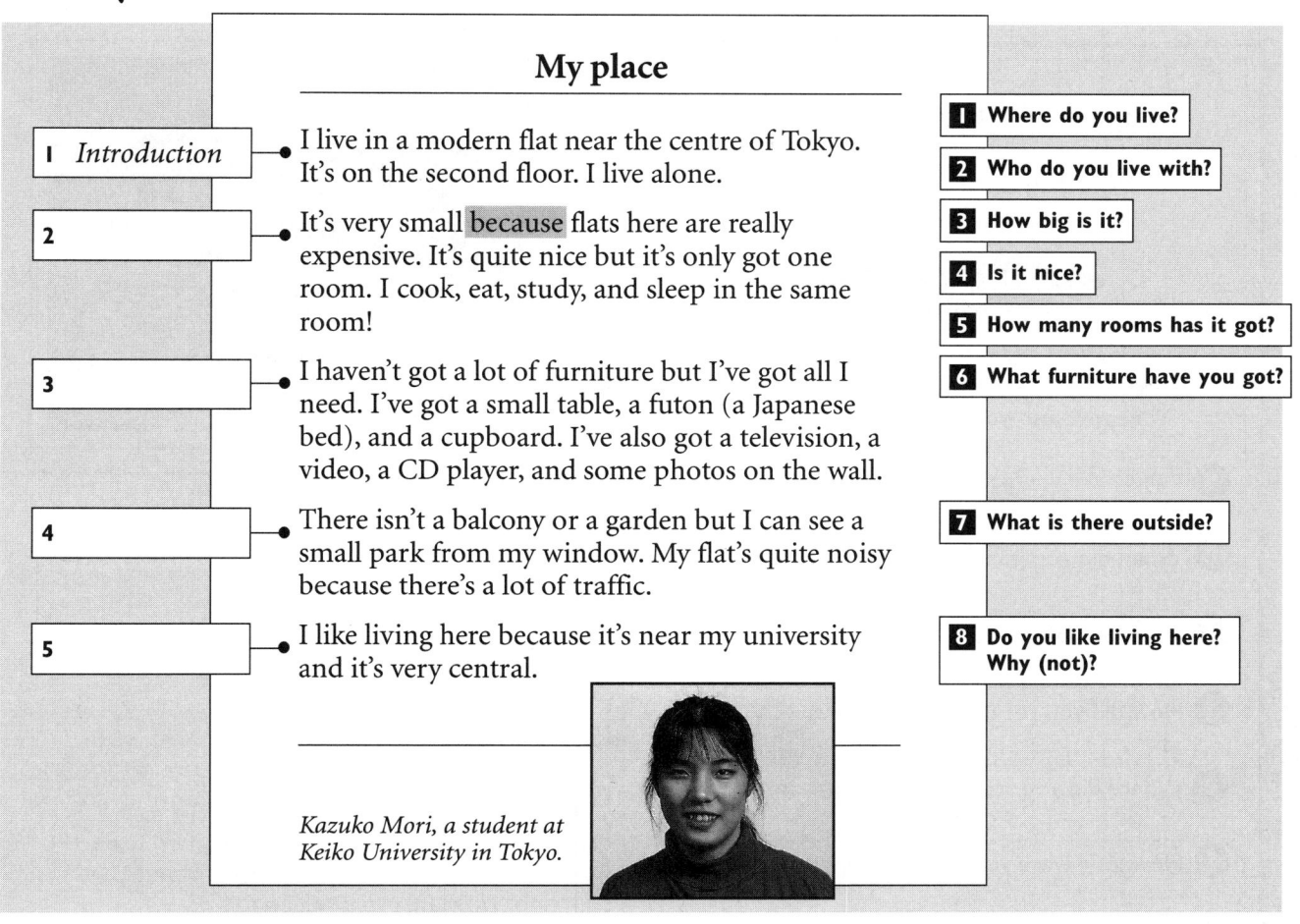

My place

1 Introduction	I live in a modern flat near the centre of Tokyo. It's on the second floor. I live alone.	**1** Where do you live? **2** Who do you live with?
2	It's very small because flats here are really expensive. It's quite nice but it's only got one room. I cook, eat, study, and sleep in the same room!	**3** How big is it? **4** Is it nice? **5** How many rooms has it got?
3	I haven't got a lot of furniture but I've got all I need. I've got a small table, a futon (a Japanese bed), and a cupboard. I've also got a television, a video, a CD player, and some photos on the wall.	**6** What furniture have you got?
4	There isn't a balcony or a garden but I can see a small park from my window. My flat's quite noisy because there's a lot of traffic.	**7** What is there outside?
5	I like living here because it's near my university and it's very central.	**8** Do you like living here? Why (not)?

Kazuko Mori, a student at Keiko University in Tokyo.

1 Read Kazuko's composition. Match paragraphs 1 to 5 with the titles.

Furniture   Outside   ~~Introduction~~
Conclusion   Room(s)

2 Right ✓ or wrong ✗?
1 She lives with a friend. ✗
2 The flat's got two bedrooms. ☐
3 She hasn't got much furniture. ☐
4 There isn't a garden. ☐
5 She lives in a quiet street. ☐
6 She doesn't like her flat. ☐

3 Match the sentence halves.

1 We live in [c]
2 He lives with ☐
3 I live ☐
4 She lives in a ☐
5 They live on ☐

a the fourth floor.
b big flat in Gdansk.
c Station Road.
d alone.
e his family.

4 **a** Highlight *because* and *but* in Kazuko's composition.

b Complete the sentences with *but* or *because*.

1 They never drive *because* their flat's near the centre.
2 I like living in the city centre _____ it's very expensive.
3 We love this street _____ all our friends live here.
4 His flat's very old _____ it's nice.
5 It's a quiet street _____ there isn't a lot of traffic.

✎ Write a composition.
- Answer questions 1 to 8.
- Write five paragraphs.
- Read and check it carefully.
- Give it to the teacher.

New words

balcony   noisy   central   outside   introduction
conclusion

Read and write

File 7

A report

A good place for a holiday

Help our readers choose a good holiday and

win £1,000!

Write a short report of a holiday you enjoyed. Answer the questionnaire. Then send us your report and your best holiday photo.

a Where did you go? To Ghana.
→

b When did you go there? In August 1992.
→

c Who did you go with? My girlfriend.
→

d How did you get there? By plane.
→

e Where did you stay? In small hotels.
→

f How long were you there? For three weeks.
→

g What did you do? Travelled around by bus.
→

h What did you see? Lovely beaches and beautiful villages.
→

i What souvenirs did you buy? Cassettes, painting, and stool.
→

j Why do you recommend it? Exciting, people friendly, and weather great.
→

Ghana

I went to Ghana in August 1992 with my girlfriend. We went by plane.

We stayed in a lot of small hotels. We were there for three weeks. We travelled around the country by bus. We saw some lovely beaches and beautiful villages. We bought some cassettes, a painting, and a stool.

I recommend it because it's exciting. The people are really friendly and the weather is great!

Toni Dolz, Madrid.

Holiday Magazine,
249 Charing Cross Road,
London WC1 3GP.

---

1 Read the questionnaire. Choose one of your holidays and answer questions a to j. (→)

2 Read Toni's report. Highlight the words in his report which are not in his answers to the questionnaire.

Now write a report of your holiday.
- Write three paragraphs.
  Paragraph 1 = questions a to d
  Paragraph 2 = questions e to i
  Paragraph 3 = question j
- Read it carefully. Check prepositions, capital letters, and full stops.
- Give it to the teacher (with a photo if you've got one).

New words

win   re**port**   **vill**age   souve**nir**   **paint**ing
stool   reco**mmend**   ex**cit**ing   **weath**er

Read and write

File 8

A postcard

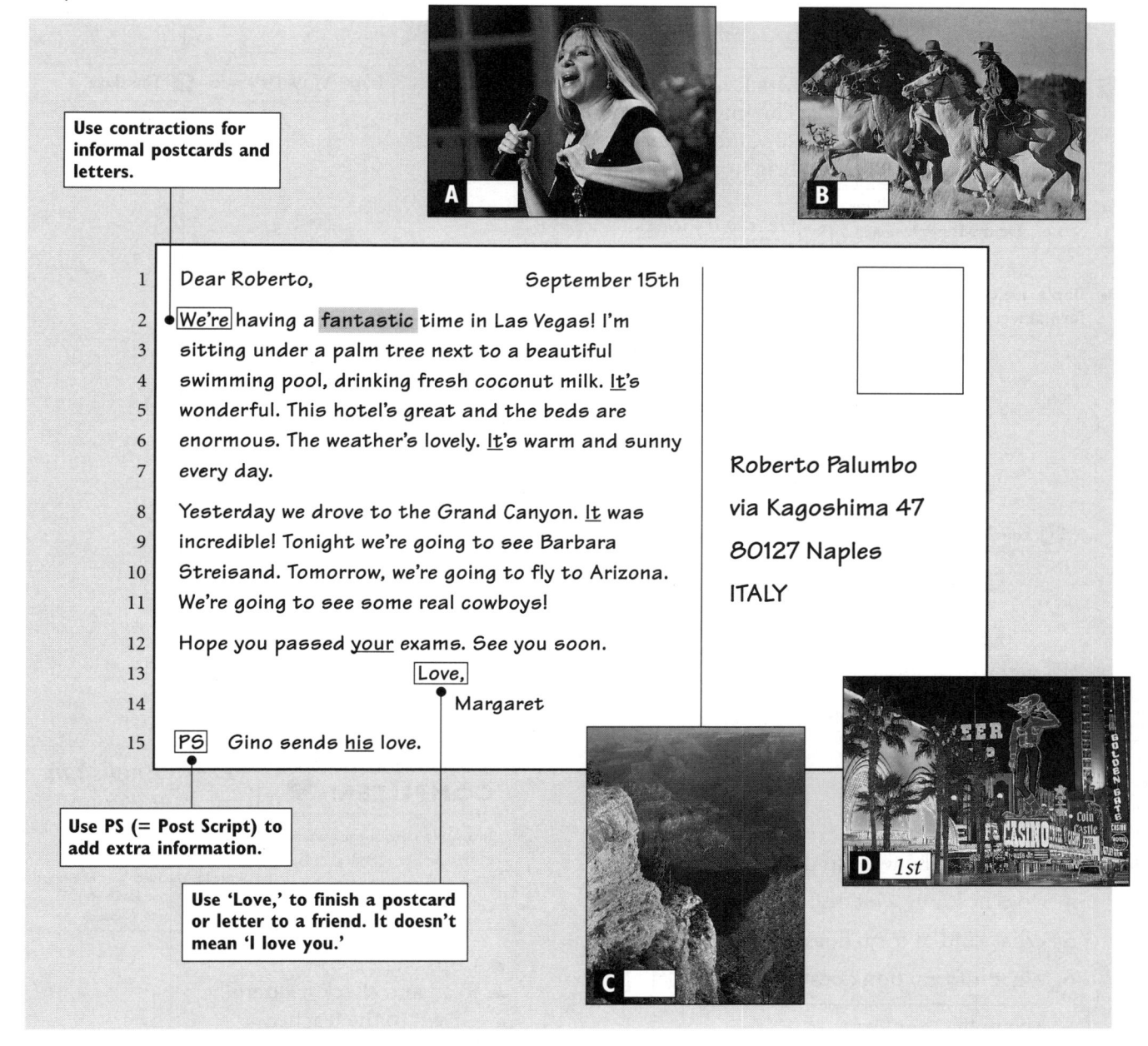

Use contractions for informal postcards and letters.

1 Dear Roberto, September 15th
2 We're having a fantastic time in Las Vegas! I'm
3 sitting under a palm tree next to a beautiful
4 swimming pool, drinking fresh coconut milk. It's
5 wonderful. This hotel's great and the beds are
6 enormous. The weather's lovely. It's warm and sunny
7 every day.
8 Yesterday we drove to the Grand Canyon. It was
9 incredible! Tonight we're going to see Barbara
10 Streisand. Tomorrow, we're going to fly to Arizona.
11 We're going to see some real cowboys!
12 Hope you passed your exams. See you soon.
13   Love,
14   Margaret
15 PS Gino sends his love.

Roberto Palumbo
via Kagoshima 47
80127 Naples
ITALY

Use PS (= Post Script) to add extra information.

Use 'Love,' to finish a postcard or letter to a friend. It doesn't mean 'I love you.'

D 1st

---

1 Read and number the photos in the right order, 1st to 4th.

2 Highlight the eleven adjectives.

3 Match the words and meanings.

1 it (line 4)   [b]
2 it (line 6)   [   ]
3 it (line 8)   [   ]
4 your (line 12) [   ]
5 his (line 15)   [   ]

a the Grand Canyon
b everything
c Roberto's
d Gino's
e the weather

Imagine an ideal place for a holiday. Imagine you're there!

- Write a postcard to another student in your class. Give this information:

  Where are you?   Yesterday
  What are you doing?   Tonight
  The weather   Tomorrow
  The hotel   Send a message

- When you finish, check your card carefully.
- Give it to the teacher.

New words

palm tree   coconut   enormous   warm   sunny
incredible   cowboy   pass *an exam*   informal

Read and write

Files 9 and 10

A formal letter

A Your address (but not your name)

6 rue du renard
Paris 75006
France

C The date

10th May 1995

B The name and address of the person you are writing to

Mrs R Jones
The International English School
23, Church Road
Brighton BN1 6GP

- Don't use initials after Dear
  NOT ~~Dear Mrs R Jones~~

- Don't use contractions in a formal letter

Dear Mrs Jones,

I am writing to ask for information about summer courses at your school.

I would like to do a course in August or September. I know a little English but not very much. Could you send me details of dates and prices, and an application form?

Could you also send me information about accommodation in Brighton?

I look forward to hearing from you.

D Finish: Yours sincerely,

Yours sincerely,

E Your signature

Jean Perrier

F Your full name

Jean Perrier

---

1 Read the letter. Match the questions and answers.

1 Who's Jean writing to? *d*
2 Why's he writing? ☐
3 When does he want to do the course? ☐
4 Does he know a lot of English? ☐
5 What kind of form does he want? ☐
6 What information does he want? ☐

a An application form.
b Dates, prices, and accommodation.
c In the summer.
d Mrs R Jones.
e No, he doesn't.
f Because he wants information.

Choose a course. Write a similar letter.

♥ **LEARN TO LOVE YOUR COMPUTER!** ♥

Intensive computer courses
Mr P Campbell (Principal),
49 Piccadilly,
London   W1V 9FL

Learn English in Canada!

Cheap classes!
Professional teachers

Write to The Easy Way to English
105 Front Street West
Toronto Canada

- Copy steps A to F.
- Read and check it carefully.
- Give it to the teacher.

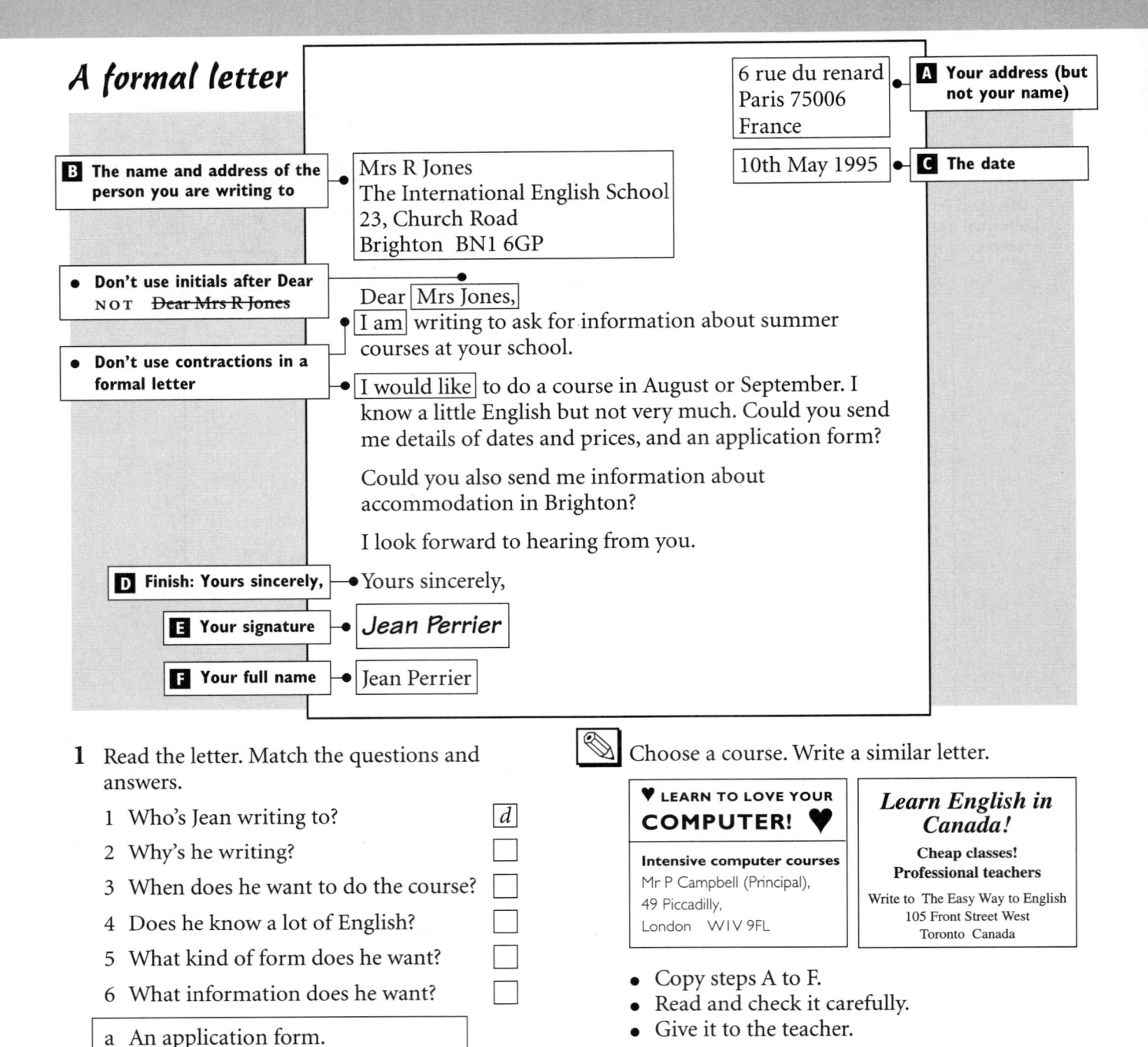

New words

signature   initials   details   application form
accommodation   look forward to
Yours sincerely

2 a Study this box.

Formal letters	Start	Finish
You don't know the name	Dear Sir / Madam	Yours faithfully
You know the name	Dear Mr / Mrs / Ms + surname	Yours sincerely

b Why does Jean's letter end *Yours sincerely* and not *Yours faithfully*?

(Circle) the right answer.

Because he **knows / doesn't know** the name of the person he's writing to.

Listen and speak

> Welcome to the 'Listen and speak' cassette.

What is it?
A cassette to help you:
- listen and speak English after class.
- practise pronunciation, vocabulary, and grammar.

Where?

In the car. On a personal stereo.  At home.

How?

Without the book, listen and:

- repeat
- translate
- imagine
- change
- answer

With the book, listen and:

- read
- check
- do a different exercise

A Here you are.
B Thank you very much.
A You're welcome.

◄◄ Listen again and repeat.

Repeat.
Yes, please.
No, thank you.
Nothing for me.
Thanks.
Coke with ice and lemon, please.
Thank you very much.

Instructions to learn

| repeat | _____ | listen (again) | _____ |
| translate | _____ | say (the negative) | _____ |

Welcome to the 'Listen and speak' cassette. Remember, after ♠ you speak.

1 A

Repeat.
EXAMPLE Hello. *Hello.*
♠
He<u>ll</u>o.
Hi!
Ex<u>c</u>use me?
S<u>o</u>rry.
Thank you.

Listen.
A Excuse me?
B Yes?
A Are you Tom Jackson?
B No, I'm not.
A Sorry.

Repeat.
Excuse me?
Yes?
Are you Tom Jackson?
No, I'm not.
Sorry.

Hi, I'm Mary White.
Nice to meet you.
Welcome to Manchester.

one two three four five six <u>se</u>ven eight nine ten

Bye! See you to<u>mo</u>rrow.
Good<u>bye</u>.

◀◀ **Listen again and translate.**

English sounds. Repeat.

/aɪ/ /aɪ/ /aɪ/ /aɪ/ Hi! nice Bye!

/m/ /m/ /m/ /m/ me meet I'm

1 B

Translate.
Good <u>mor</u>ning.
Good af<u>ter</u>noon.
Good <u>e</u>vening.
Good night.

◀◀ **Listen again and repeat.**

Repeat.
A B C D E F G H I J K L M
N O P Q R S T U V W X Y Z

Listen.
A Good afternoon. What's your name?
B My name's Lee.
A Sorry? How do you spell it?
B L-double E.

A Where are you from?
B I'm from Hong Kong.
A You're in room 10.

Repeat.
What's your name?
My name's Lee.
Sorry?
How do you spell it?

◀◀ **Listen again and translate.**

1 C

Repeat.
He's <u>Bri</u>tish.
He isn't <u>A</u>merican.
Where's he from?
He's from <u>Man</u>chester.

She's <u>I</u>talian.
She isn't <u>S</u>panish.
Where's she from?
She's from Mi<u>lan</u>.

Say the negative.
EXAMPLE You're German. *You aren't German.*
♠
You're German.   You aren't German.
He's French.   He isn't French.
She's Spanish.   She isn't Spanish.
I'm British.   I'm not British.

Repeat.
What's his name?
His name's Julio.
What's her name?
Her name's Sophia.

◀◀ **Listen again and translate.**

English sounds. Repeat.

/e/ /e/ /e/ /e/ yes spell
Ten French hotels.

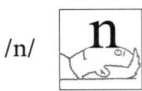

/n/ /n/ /n/ /n/ nine banana
I don't know.

1 D

Repeat.
What's this?
It's a camera.
Is it a video camera?
Yes, it is.
Is it your camera?
No, it isn't.

◀◀ **Listen again and translate.**

Listen.
A Excuse me, please. What's this in English?
B It's a ball.
A How do you spell it?
B B-A-double L.
A How do you pronounce it?
B Ball.

Repeat.
What's this in English?
How do you spell it?
How do you pronounce it?

◄◄ **Listen again and translate.**

Translate.
Stand up.
Sit down.
Open your book.
Don't write.
Read the instructions.
Close your book.

◄◄ **Listen again and repeat.**

English sounds. Repeat.

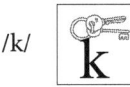

/k/   /k/ /k/ /k/   close   book   car park

/ɪ/   /ɪ/ /ɪ/ /ɪ/   in   his
             Six English videos.

1 E

Repeat.
Monday
Tuesday
Wednesday
Thursday
Friday
Saturday
Sunday

◄◄ **Close your book and remember the days.**

Listen.
A Good evening. Are you American?
B No, we aren't.
A Are you English?
B Yes, we are. We're English.

Repeat.
Yes, we are.
No, we aren't.
We're English.

Listen.
A Are they Spanish?
B No, they aren't.
A Are they Italian?
B Yes, they are. They're Italian.

◄◄ **Listen again and translate.**

Repeat.
I'm   – I'm not
you're   – you aren't
he's   – he isn't
she's   – she isn't
it's   – it isn't
we're   – we aren't
they're – they aren't

e<u>le</u>ven   twelve   thir<u>teen</u>   four<u>teen</u>   fif<u>teen</u>   six<u>teen</u>
seven<u>teen</u>   eigh<u>teen</u>   nine<u>teen</u>   <u>twen</u>ty   twenty-<u>one</u>

◄◄ **Close your book and say the numbers.**

English sounds. Repeat.

/iː/   /iː/ /iː/ /iː/   be   three
             We speak Greek.

1

Listen.
A Good morning. Anything to drink, sir?
B Coffee, please.
A Milk and sugar?
B Milk, no sugar.
A Here you are.
B Thank you very much.
A You're welcome.

◄◄ **Listen again and repeat.**

Repeat.
Yes, please.
No, thank you.
Nothing for me.
Thanks.
Coke with ice and lemon, please.
Thank you very much.
You're welcome.

◄◄ **Listen again and translate.**

2 A

Repeat.
What's this?
It's an umbrella.
What are these?
They're keys.

◄◄ **Listen again and translate.**

English sounds. Repeat.

/s/   /s/ /s/ /s/

/z/   /z/ /z/ /z/

Say the plural.

EXAMPLES a window *windows*
a case *cases*

a <u>win</u>dow   windows /z/
a case   cases /ɪz/
a book   books /s/
an <u>o</u>range   oranges /ɪz/
a chair   chairs /z/
a <u>wa</u>llet   wallets /s/

◄◄ **Listen again and repeat.**

Repeat.

<u>thir</u>ty <u>thir</u>ty-three <u>for</u>ty-four <u>fif</u>ty-five <u>six</u>ty-six
<u>se</u>venty-<u>se</u>ven <u>eigh</u>ty-eight <u>nine</u>ty-nine a <u>hun</u>dred
a <u>hun</u>dred and one

◄◄ **Listen again and write the numbers.**

2 B

Listen.

A Where's the file?
B It's on the table.
A And where are the pens?
B They're in the drawer.

◄◄ **Listen again and translate.**

Ask the question.

EXAMPLES the clock *Where's the clock?*
the desks *Where are the desks?*

the clock   Where's the clock?
the desks   Where are the desks?
the bin   Where's the bin?
the keys   Where are the keys?

Answer.

EXAMPLES Are the keys on the floor? *Yes, they are.*
Is the cat under the table? *Yes, it is.*

Are the keys on the floor?   Yes, they are.
Is the cat under the table?   Yes, it is.
Is the phone in your room?   Yes, it is.
Are the pens in your bag?   Yes, they are.

◄◄ **Listen again and repeat the questions.**

English sounds. Repeat.

/ɔː/   /ɔː/ /ɔː/ /ɔː/ **four forty**
The **door**, the **wall**, and the **floor**.

/ð/   /ð/ /ð/ /ð/ **the there**
This, **that**, **these**, and **those**.

2 C

Finish the sentence.

EXAMPLE In Italy *they speak Italian.*

In <u>I</u>taly   they speak Italian.
In France   they speak French.
In <u>Ru</u>ssia   they speak Russian.
In Spain   they speak Spanish.

◄◄ **Listen again and translate.**

Say the negative.

EXAMPLE I understand. *I don't understand.*

I understand.   I don't understand.
I speak Japanese.   I don't speak Japanese.
I like rock music.   I don't like rock music.
We play tennis.   We don't play tennis.

Repeat.

Do you speak German?
Do you play tennis?
Do you like football?
Do you speak English?

◄◄ **Listen again and answer *Yes, I do.* or *No, I don't.***

English sounds. Repeat.

/ʌ/   /ʌ/ /ʌ/ /ʌ/ c**o**me **u**nder
I st**u**dy R**u**ssian on M**o**ndays.

/d/   /d/ /d/ /d/ **d**o **d**ay
I **d**on't un**d**erstan**d**.

2 D

Repeat.

one – first
two – second
three – third
four – fourth
five – fifth
six – sixth

◄◄ **Close your book and remember the numbers.**

English sounds. Repeat.

/ə/   comput**er** com****t**er** comput**er**
/ə/ /ə/ /ə/ th**e** wat**er**
A pizz**a** and **a** banan**a**.

/w/   /w/ /w/ /w/ **w**hen **W**ednesday
What a **w**onderful **w**orld

Repeat.
What do you do?
I'm a <u>doc</u>tor.
He's a <u>jour</u>nalist.
She's a <u>ma</u>nager.
We're <u>stu</u>dents.

◄◄ **Listen again and translate.**

Listen.
A Do you work?
B Yes, I do.
A What do you do?
B I'm a secretary.
A Oh. And do you study?
B Yes, I do. I study French.
A Do you like your course?
B It's OK.

◄◄ **Listen again and translate.**

2

Repeat.
Can I change $100, please?
Do you have a pen?
Just a moment.
Here you are.

Listen.
A Good afternoon, sir.
B Hello. Can I have a steak sandwich, please?
A Anything else?
B Yes. A large apple juice. How much is that?

◄◄ **Listen again and translate.**

Ask the question.
EXAMPLE an apple juice   *Can I have an apple juice, please?*

an <u>a</u>pple juice   Can I have an apple juice, please?
a <u>sand</u>wich   Can I have a sandwich, please?
a <u>cheese</u>burger   Can I have a cheeseburger, please?

Repeat.
How much is a coffee?
How much are chips?
How much are sandwiches?
How much is an orange juice?

◄◄ **Listen again and translate.**

3 A

Change the sentence.
EXAMPLE I smoke.   *She smokes.*

I smoke.   She smokes.
I study.   She studies.
I live in a flat. She lives in a flat.
I watch TV.   She watches TV.

Repeat.
I don't drink coffee.
He doesn't drink coffee.
I don't speak Spanish.
He doesn't speak Spanish.

Repeat.
Does Catherine live in a house?
Yes, she does.
Does she speak French?
No, she doesn't.
Does Terry work in a hotel?
No, he doesn't.
Does he play football?
Yes, he does.

◄◄ **Listen again and translate.**

English sounds. Repeat.

/æ/   /æ/ /æ/ /æ/ have thanks
      That's my bag.

/v/   /v/ /v/ /v/ love very
      A video in the evening.

◄◄ **Sound bank *p.81/2* Practise /æ/ and /v/.**

3 B

Remember.
Natasha lives in Sydney. She's a journalist. She plays volleyball. She likes rock music and she drives a Ferrari.

Answer.
EXAMPLE Where does Natasha live?   *She lives in Sydney.*

Where does Natasha live?   She lives in Sydney.
What does she do?   She's a journalist.
What sports does she play?   She plays volleyball.
What music does she like?   She likes rock music.
What car does she drive?   She drives a Ferrari.

◄◄ **Listen again and repeat the questions.**

English sounds. Repeat.

/eə/   /eə/ /eə/ /eə/ th**ere** Hungarian
       Wh**ere**'s the **air**port?

/f/   /f/ /f/ /f/ **F**riday o**ff**ice
       Fi**f**ty-**f**ive **ph**otos.

◄◄ **Sound bank *p.81/2* Practise /eə/ and /f/.**

3 C

English sounds. Repeat.

/ɑː/ /ɑː/ /ɑː/ /ɑː/ answer aren't Charles can't dance.

/dʒ/ /dʒ/ /dʒ/ /dʒ/ Japan Germany orange juice

◀◀ **Sound bank** *p.81/2* **Practise /ɑː/ and /dʒ/.**

Repeat.
Can you type?
Yes, I can.
I can type quite well.
Can you use a computer?
No, I can't.

Say *positive* or *negative*.
EXAMPLES He can drive. *positive*
          We can't dance. *negative*

He can drive.   positive
We can't dance.   negative
I can ski.   positive
She can't swim.   negative
They can sing very well. positive

◀◀ **Listen again and translate.**

3 D

Translate.
a second
a minute
an hour
a day
a week
a month
a year

◀◀ **Close your book and remember the seven words.**

Repeat.
What's the time?
It's one o'clock.
It's a quarter past two.
It's half past three.
It's a quarter to four.

◀◀ **Listen again and translate.**

English sounds. Repeat.

/ɒ/ /ɒ/ /ɒ/ /ɒ/ what sorry Stop! I want a hot dog.

/ɜː/ /ɜː/ /ɜː/ /ɜː/ work thirsty 'First' and 'third' are English words.

◀◀ **Sound bank** *p.81/2* **Practise /ɒ/ and /ɜː/.**

3

Listen.
A Do you have any rooms, please?
B Would you like a single room?
A Yes, please.
B With or without a bathroom?
A With.
B How many nights would you like to stay?
A How much is it a night?
B £50, including breakfast.
A That's fine. Two nights, please.

◀◀ **Listen again and translate.**

Repeat.
Do you have any rooms, please?
Would you like a single room?
How much is it a night?
That's fine. Two nights, please.

◀◀ **Listen again and translate.**

Check into a hotel. Answer.
Good evening. Would you like a single room or a double room? 🔔
With or without a bathroom? 🔔
And how many nights would you like to stay? 🔔
That's fine. Can I see your passport, please? 🔔

4 A

Translate.
black blue brown green grey orange pink purple red white yellow

◀◀ **Close your book and remember the eleven colours.**

Repeat.
It's a big house.
They're very expensive.
She's a tall girl.
He's a nice man.
We're very tired.
Is he a good actor?

◀◀ **Listen again and translate.**

Say the opposite.
EXAMPLES big *small*
          good *bad*

big   small
good   bad
hot   cold
expensive   cheap
easy   difficult
fast   slow
sad   happy

72

English sounds. Repeat.

/j/ /j/ /j/ /j/ year yellow
You're young and beautiful.

/u:/ /u:/ /u:/ /u:/ who food
New blue boots.

◂◂ Sound bank *p.81/2* Practise /j/ and /u:/.

4 B

Say the female.
EXAMPLES man *woman*
          son *daughter*

man	woman
son	daughter
father	mother
boy	girl
brother	sister
husband	wife
boyfriend	girlfriend

◂◂ Close your books and remember the fourteen words.

Say the plural.
EXAMPLE wife *wives*

wife	wives
man	men
woman	women
person	people
child	children

Translate.
Horatio is Hamlet's friend.
McDonald's hamburgers.
This is my father's car.
These are my sister's jeans.
Is it your mother's house?

◂◂ Listen again and repeat.

4 C

English sounds. Repeat.

/h/ /h/ /h/ /h/ happy hotel
Help! Her husband's here.

/g/ /g/ /g/ /g/ golf again
I've got a green guitar.

◂◂ Sound bank *p.81/2* Practise /h/ and /g/.

Make a sentence.
EXAMPLE I *I've got a car.*

I	I've got a car.
he	He's got a car.
she	She's got a car.
we	We've got a car.

Say the negative.
EXAMPLE I *I haven't got any sisters.*

I	I haven't got any sisters.
he	He hasn't got any sisters.
she	She hasn't got any sisters.
they	They haven't got any sisters.

Ask the question.
EXAMPLES a bike *Have you got a bike?*
         photos *Have you got any photos?*

a bike	Have you got a bike?
photos	Have you got any photos?
matches	Have you got any matches?
a fax	Have you got a fax?

◂◂ Listen again and answer *Yes, I have.* or *No, I haven't.*

4 D

English sounds. Repeat.

/ŋ/ /ŋ/ /ŋ/ /ŋ/ thing uncle
Thanks for the drink.

/ʊ/ /ʊ/ /ʊ/ /ʊ/ put sugar
A good-looking woman.

◂◂ Sound bank *p.81/2* Practise /ŋ/ and /ʊ/.

Repeat.
I love travelling.
He likes skiing very much.
She doesn't like swimming very much.
We don't like working.
John hates dancing.

◂◂ Listen again and translate.

Ask the question.
EXAMPLE study English *Do you like studying English?*

study English	Do you like studying English?
play chess	Do you like playing chess?
watch TV	Do you like watching TV?
listen to music	Do you like listening to music?

Repeat.
Yes, I do. I love it.
It's all right.
No, not much.
No, I don't. I hate it!

◂◂ Listen again and answer the questions.

4

Repeat.
Could I have ten stamps for Europe, please?
Thanks a lot.
Have you got any envelopes?
How much is the guidebook?
And how much are the postcards?

◀◀ **Listen again and translate.**

Ask the question.
EXAMPLE a toothbrush *Could I have a toothbrush, please?*

a toothbrush   Could I have a toothbrush, please?
a pencil   Could I have a pencil, please?
two batteries Could I have two batteries, please?

5 A

Change the sentence.
EXAMPLE I go *he goes*

I go   he goes
I don't go   he doesn't go
I start work   he starts work
I use   he uses
I don't study   he doesn't study

Repeat.
She gets up late.
She has a shower.
She doesn't have breakfast.
She goes to work by car.
She has lunch at half past one.
She finishes work at six o'clock.
She gets home late.
After that she watches TV.
She goes to bed very late.

◀◀ **Listen again and translate.**

English sounds. Repeat.

/ɔɪ/   /ɔɪ/ /ɔɪ/ /ɔɪ/ toilet royal
       My boyfriend's unemployed.

/b/   /b/ /b/ /b/ blue rubber
       My boyfriend's big brother.

◀◀ **Sound bank *p.81/2* Practise /ɔɪ/ and /b/.**

5 B

Repeat.
I always get up early.
I usually have three meals a day.
I often put salt on food.
I sometimes drink coffee.
I hardly ever go out.
I never take sugar in tea.

◀◀ **Listen again and translate.**

Translate.
Do you often eat fried food?
Yes, I do.
And do you often do exercise?
No, I don't.

Repeat.
Do you often eat fried food?
Do you often do exercise?
Do you often travel by car?
Do you often drink alcohol?

◀◀ **Listen again and answer *Yes, I do.* or *No, I don't.***

English sounds. Repeat.

/ɪə/   /ɪə/ /ɪə/ /ɪə/ here year
       We're near the museum.

/ʃ/   /ʃ/ /ʃ/ /ʃ/ shop finish
       She uses Russian sugar.

◀◀ **Sound bank *p.81/2* Practise /ɪə/ and /ʃ/. Close your book. How many words can you remember?**

5 C

Listen.
A How often do you eat fresh fruit?
B About once a month. And I like playing golf.
A Yes? How often do you play golf?
B About once a year.

Repeat.
How often do you play golf?
How often do you cook?
How often do you walk?
How often do you travel?

◀◀ **Listen again and answer the questions.**

Say *in*, *on*, or *at*.

EXAMPLES the weekend *at the weekend*
the morning *in the morning*

the wee<u>k</u>end	at the weekend
the <u>mor</u>ning	in the morning
<u>Tues</u>day	on Tuesday
the <u>sum</u>mer	in the summer
<u>Christ</u>mas	at Christmas
the after<u>noon</u>	in the afternoon
<u>Fri</u>day <u>eve</u>ning	on Friday evening
night	at night

◀◀ **Listen again and do it without a mistake.**

Translate.
once a day
twice a week
three times a month
four times a year
every day

◀◀ **Listen again and repeat.**

English sounds. Repeat.

/t/   /t/ /t/ /t/ **t**all le**tt**er
Twen**t**y-**t**wo **t**ired s**t**uden**t**s.

/aʊ/   /aʊ/ /aʊ/ /aʊ/ n**ow** th**ou**sand
Our h**ou**se is br**ow**n.

◀◀ **Sound bank *p.81/2* Practise /t/ and /aʊ/.**

5

Say *waiter* or *customer*.
EXAMPLES A table for two, please. *customer*
Are you ready to order now? *waiter*

A table for two, please.	customer
Are you ready to order now?	waiter
I'd like chicken soup, please.	customer
And for your main course?	waiter
Could I have fish and chips?	customer
Anything to drink?	waiter
Have you got a light?	customer
Would you like anything else?	waiter
Could I have the bill, please?	customer
Can I pay by credit card?	customer

◀◀ **Listen again and repeat.**

6 A

Say *positive* or *negative*.
EXAMPLES They're brilliant. *positive*
It's terrible. *negative*

They're <u>bril</u>liant.	positive
It's <u>terr</u>ible.	negative
He's <u>bor</u>ing.	negative
She's great.	positive
That's <u>love</u>ly.	positive

◀◀ **Listen again and repeat.**

Ask the question.
EXAMPLES We hate pop music. *Why do you hate it?*
I hate jeans. *Why do you hate them?*

We hate pop music.	Why do you hate it?
I hate jeans.	Why do you hate them?
We hate Madonna.	Why do you hate her?
I hate André Agassi.	Why do you hate him?
We hate classical music.	Why do you hate it?

◀◀ **Listen again and imagine answers with *Because* ....**

English sounds. Repeat.

/tʃ/   /tʃ/ /tʃ/ /tʃ/ **ch**eap wa**tch**
Cheese, **ch**ips, and **ch**ocolate for lun**ch**!

/eɪ/   /eɪ/ /eɪ/ /eɪ/ M**ay** w**ai**t
Eight d**ay**s in Sp**ai**n.

◀◀ **Sound bank *p.81/2* Practise /tʃ/ and /eɪ/. Close your book. Choose and spell ten words.**

6 B

Listen.
A We've got a new flat.
B Oh, great. Is it nice?
A Yes, very nice. There's a big kitchen and there are two large bedrooms.
B Is there a garage?
A No, there isn't.

Ask the question.
EXAMPLES a garage *Is there a garage?*
plants *Are there any plants?*

a <u>ga</u>rage?	Is there a garage?
plants	Are there any plants?
chairs	Are there any chairs?
a <u>gar</u>den	Is there a garden?

◀◀ **Listen again and answer *Yes* or *No* for your flat.**

Repeat.
There's a kitchen,
and there are two bedrooms.
There are some plants,
but there aren't any pictures.

◀◀ **Listen again and translate.**

6 C

Listen.
A Where were you last night?
B I was at home.
A Were you alone?
B Yes, I was.

Repeat.
Where were you last night?
Where were you last Wednesday?
Where were you last weekend?
Where were you yesterday afternoon?

◀◀ **Listen again and translate.**

Say *at* or *in*.
EXAMPLES school   *I was at school.*
          bed   *I was in bed.*

school	I was at school.
bed	I was in bed.
home	I was at home.
the kitchen	I was in the kitchen.
work	I was at work.

Say the negative.
EXAMPLES He was alone. *He wasn't alone.*
          We were late. *We weren't late.*

He was a<u>lone</u>.	He wasn't alone.
We were late.	We weren't late.
She was <u>hun</u>gry.	She wasn't hungry.
They were <u>an</u>gry.	They weren't angry.

◀◀ **Listen again and translate.**

English sounds. Repeat.

/r/   /r/ /r/ /r/ run wrong
      Happy Christmas everybody!

Silent /r/   Here, there,
             Near, far,
             You're sure to find
             A silent /r/.

◀◀ **Sound bank *p.81/2* Practise /r/ and silent /r/. Listen again and learn the poem.**

6 D

Say the past simple.
EXAMPLE There's a knife. *There was a knife.*

There's a knife.	There was a knife.
There are some papers.	There were some papers.
There isn't a gun.	There wasn't a gun.
There aren't any chairs.	There weren't any chairs.

Listen.
A Police! Help! I can't find my bag!
B Don't worry, madam. What was in your bag? Were there any credit cards?
A No, there weren't.
B Was there a purse?
A Yes, there was. With all my money.

◀◀ **Listen again and translate.**

Repeat.
Yes, there was.
No, there wasn't.
Yes, there were.
No, there weren't.

6

Listen.
A Hello. Do you speak English?
B Yes, I do. Can I help you?
A Yes, please. We'd like to go to Barcelona on Tuesday.
B By bus, train, or plane?
A What time does the first train leave?

◀◀ **Listen again and translate.**

Repeat.
We'd like to go to Barcelona on Tuesday.
What time does the first train leave?
What time does it arrive?

7 A

Make the sentence in the past simple.
EXAMPLES go shopping   *I went shopping.*
          have a shower *I had a shower.*

go <u>shop</u>ping	I went shopping.
have a <u>show</u>er	I had a shower.
go to the bank	I went to the bank.
have <u>break</u>fast	I had breakfast.

◀◀ **Listen again and translate.**

Ask the question.
EXAMPLE go out *Did you go out last night?*

go out	Did you go out last night?
have dinner	Did you have dinner last night?
go to the cinema	Did you go to the cinema last night?
have a drink	Did you have a drink last night?

◀◀ **Listen again and answer *Yes, I did.* or *No, I didn't*.**

Say the negative.
EXAMPLE a cigarette *I didn't have a cigarette.*

a cigarette	I didn't have a cigarette.
to the hairdresser's	I didn't go to the hairdresser's.
lunch	I didn't have lunch.
to the gym	I didn't go to the gym.

English sounds. Repeat.

/əʊ/   /əʊ/ /əʊ/ /əʊ/ cl<u>o</u>se <u>o</u>pen
       Oh no! Don't go home.

/ʒ/   /ʒ/ /ʒ/ /ʒ/ u<u>s</u>ually revi<u>s</u>ion
       An unu<u>s</u>ual gara<u>g</u>e.

◀◀ **Sound bank *p.81/2* Practise /əʊ/. Close your book. Choose and spell six words.**

7 B

Repeat.
cook – cooked
dance – danced
watch – watched
play – played
<u>stu</u>dy – <u>stu</u>died

read – read
get – got
buy – bought
see – saw
meet – met

Say the past simple.
EXAMPLE I do *I did*

I do	I did
I stay	I stayed
I walk	I walked
I get	I got
I read	I read
I dance	I danced

◀◀ **Listen again and repeat.**

Repeat.
Did you go out last week?
Where did you go?
Who did you go with?
Did you have a good time?

◀◀ **Listen again and answer.**

7 C

English sounds. Repeat.

/θ/   /θ/ /θ/ /θ/ **th**in ba**th**
Thir**t**y-**th**ree **Th**ursdays.

◀◀ **Sound bank *p.81/2* Practise /θ/.**

Repeat.
<u>Ja</u>nuary <u>Fe</u>bruary March <u>A</u>pril May June Ju<u>ly</u> <u>Au</u>gust Sep<u>tem</u>ber Oc<u>to</u>ber No<u>vem</u>ber De<u>cem</u>ber

◀◀ **Close your book and say the months.**

Say the next number.
EXAMPLE first, second, *third*

first, <u>se</u>cond,   third
fifth, sixth,   <u>se</u>venth
thir<u>teenth</u>, four<u>teenth</u>,   fif<u>teenth</u>
eigh<u>teenth</u>, nine<u>teenth</u>, <u>twen</u>tieth
twenty-<u>se</u>cond, twenty-<u>third</u>, twenty-<u>fourth</u>

Repeat.
3rd July 1980
20th April 1854
19th November 1995
31st December 1999

◀◀ **Close your book. Listen again and write the dates.**

Repeat.
What's the date today?
What year is it?
When's your birthday?
When were you born?

◀◀ **Listen again and answer.**

7 D

Repeat.
She typed a letter. /t/
She packed a case. /t/
She called a taxi. /d/
She arrived at the airport. /d/
The plane landed. /ɪd/
She waited for six hours. /ɪd/

◀◀ **Listen again and translate.**

Say *present* or *past*.
EXAMPLES I want a new car. *present*
          I wanted a new car. *past*

I want a new car.	present
I wanted a new car.	past
She smokes.	present
He worked in a bank.	past
I stayed in last night.	past
We live near here.	present
He waited for two hours.	past

◀◀ **Listen again and repeat.**

7 🛄

Repeat.
Excuse me. Where's the market?
Is there a market near here?
Could you tell me the way to the market, please?
Could you say that again, please?
Could you speak more slowly, please?
Could you show me on the map?

◀◀ **Listen again and translate.**

Translate.
Turn left.
Turn right.
Turn right at the traffic lights.
Go straight on.
Go past the school.
It's on the left.

◀◀ **Listen again and repeat.**

77

8 A

Say the negative.
EXAMPLE They're talking. *They aren't talking.*

They're talking.	They aren't talking.
She's running.	She isn't running.
I'm working.	I'm not working.
It's raining.	It isn't raining.

Ask the question.
EXAMPLE learn English *Are you learning English?*

learn English	Are you learning English?
have a party	Are you having a party?
cook dinner	Are you cooking dinner?
listen to music	Are you listening to music?

◄◄ **Listen again and answer *Yes, I am.* or *No, I'm not.***

Ask the question.
EXAMPLE he *What's he doing?*

he	What's he doing?
you	What are you doing?
they	What are they doing?
she	What's she doing?

◄◄ **Listen again and translate.**

8 B

Translate.
a dress   a hat   a jacket   a shirt   shoes   a skirt   socks
a suit   a sweater   trainers   trousers

◄◄ **Close your book and remember the eleven clothes words.**

Answer *yes* or *no*.
Do you work?
Are you working now?
Do you wear perfume?
Are you wearing perfume now?
Do you read the paper every day?
Are you reading the paper now?

◄◄ **Listen again and answer *Yes, I am. / No, I'm not.* or *Yes, I do. / No, I don't.***

English sounds. Repeat.

/p/   /p/ /p/ /p/   people   passport
A perfect piece of pizza.

/l/   /l/ /l/ /l/   lunch   follow
I love living in Liverpool.

◄◄ **Sound bank *p.81/2* Practise /p/ and /l/.**

8 C

Say the sentence.
EXAMPLES she *She's going to have a party.*
we *We're going to have a party.*

she	She's going to have a party.
we	We're going to have a party.
they	They're going to have a party.
I	I'm going to have a party.
he	He's going to have a party.

Ask the question.
EXAMPLE buy a new car *Are you going to buy a new car?*

buy a new car	Are you going to buy a new car?
study tonight	Are you going to study tonight?
work tomorrow	Are you going to work tomorrow?
see a film tonight	Are you going to see a film tonight?

◄◄ **Listen again and answer *Yes, I am.* or *No, I'm not.***

Translate.
What are you going to do tonight?
Who are you going to meet this weekend?
Where are you going to go this summer?

◄◄ **Listen again and repeat. Imagine your answers.**

8

Listen.
A Good morning. Can I help you?
B Could I speak to David, please?
A One moment, please. Sorry, it's engaged. Would you like to hold?
B Yes, OK.
A I'm sorry. It's still engaged.
B I'll call back later.

Repeat.
Could I speak to David, please?
One moment, please.
It's engaged.
I'll call back later.
Hello. Is that David?
Speaking.
Hi! This is Jenny.

◄◄ **Listen again and translate.**

9 A

Repeat.
quick – quicker
slow – slower
happy – happier
important – more important
dangerous – less dangerous

◄◄ **Listen again and translate.**

Say the comparative.
new   newer
easy   easier
beautiful more beautiful
good   better
bad   worse
difficult more difficult

◄◄ **Listen again and say the opposite comparative.**

Say *true* or *false*.
EXAMPLE London is larger than Moscow. *true*

London is larger than Moscow.   true
Germany is hotter than Egypt.   false
Faxes are faster than letters.   true
Elephants are smaller than dogs.   false
Bikes are more expensive than cars. false

◄◄ **Listen again and correct the false sentences.**

9 B

Say the negative.
EXAMPLE We're going to win. *We aren't going to win.*

We're going to win.   We aren't going to win.
He's going to lose.   He isn't going to lose.
They're going to travel. They aren't going to travel.
It's going to rain.   It isn't going to rain.

◄◄ **Listen again and translate.**

Translate.
Are you going to get married next year?
I think so.
I hope so.
Maybe.
I don't think so.
I hope not.

◄◄ **Listen again and repeat the answers.**

Answer.
Are you going to move house this year?
Are you going to retire soon?
Are you going to have a lot of children?
Are you going to travel round the world?
Are you going to study English next year?

◄◄ **Listen again and repeat the questions.**

9 C

Say the adverb.
EXAMPLES quick *quickly*
         beautiful *beautifully*

quick   quickly
beautiful beautifully
bad   badly
careful   carefully
easy   easily
good   well

◄◄ **Listen again and do it without a mistake.**

Answer *true* or *false*.
You drive badly.
You speak quickly.
You walk very slowly.
You play football quite well.
You cook beautifully.

9 D

Imagine.
a kilo of spaghetti
500 grams of butter
a tin of tomatoes
a bottle of white wine
a small box of mushrooms

◄◄ **Listen again and repeat.**

Make a sentence.
EXAMPLES oil / no *We don't need any oil.*
         chicken / yes *We need some chicken.*

oil / no   We don't need any oil.
chicken / yes   We need some chicken.
cheese / yes   We need some cheese.
mushrooms / no   We don't need any mushrooms.
tomatoes / yes   We need some tomatoes.

◄◄ **Listen again and do it without a mistake.**

Ask the question.
EXAMPLES pasta *How much pasta would you like?*
         carrots *How many carrots would you like?*

pasta   How much pasta would you like?
carrots How many carrots would you like?
eggs   How many eggs would you like?
rice   How much rice would you like?
chips   How many chips would you like?

◄◄ **Listen again and translate.**

9

Listen.

A Good morning. Can I help you, madam?
B Yes. Have you got this shirt in black?
A Yes. What size are you?
B I'm not sure. Medium, I think.
A Just a moment … This is medium.
B Can I try it on?
A Of course. The changing rooms are over there.

A Is it all right?
B Hm. It's a bit too big.
A Try this one. It's smaller.
B OK. I'll take it. Can I pay by cheque?
A Yes, of course.

◀◀ **Listen again and translate.**

Repeat.

Have you got this shirt in black?
What size are you?
Can I try it on?
It's a bit too big.
OK. I'll take it.
Can I pay by cheque?

◀◀ **Listen again and answer the questions.**

Translate.

What would you like to drink?
Anything else?
Would you like a single room or a double room?
Could I have a stamp, please?
Have you got a light?
What time does your English class start?
Could you say that again, please?
What's your phone number?

◀◀ **Listen again and answer the questions.**

Sound bank

Practise English sounds. Repeat, spell, and remember the words.

Vowels

aɪ hi fine five like nice night write my why bye
I Y

e pen yes desk help when tell spell stress twelve French
F L M N S X Z

ɪ it in his six film milk this with sing think

iː be he read please speak three Greece key ski piece
B C D E G P T V

ɔː or for sport four your you're board door small talk

ʌ one bus but cup club just much lunch come love

ə a pizza Brazil again America banana camera cassette today tomorrow actor doctor the

ɜː her verb girl first third word work world learn nurse

æ am at bag man bank have that black stand thanks

eə hair pair where there wear their they're

ɑː ask bar park star start large class dance France are
R

ɒ on hot not job from rock stop wrong want what

uː do who too food school you use new two blue juice
Q U W

ʊ put full book cook good look room could would

ɔɪ oil point noise voice royal unemployed

ɪə dear hear near real here we're

aʊ how now town brown our hour noun count pound sound

eɪ date name take page change plane eight Spain they day
A H J K

əʊ no go cold close smoke don't home road know
O

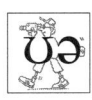

ʊə tour plural pure Europe

Consonants

m — meet woman camera shampoo tomorrow information I'm summer welcome

n — not nice banana pronunciation nine man tennis know

k — car park clock capital contraction communication chocolate look taxi

dʒ — job jeans January Germany manager imagine age orange

w — water worry window Wednesday twenty-one what where question

s — stops starts sister six asks lesson city police

z — zoo music easy is days eyes pens use these please

d — day date dance drink down study understand address

ð — the they there this that those father brother

v — very vowel seven have five love of

f — first Friday fifty-five after before office coffee photo

j — your year young yellow yesterday use university beautiful

h — his her how high hotel hungry behind who

g — good golf great again angry flag egg guitar

ŋ — language singing thing song morning drink think bank

b — bad buy birthday baby table problem job rubber

ʃ — sure sugar tissue she shop finish station washing machine

t — ten tall time stop style city student night letter cassette

tʃ — cheap chips cheese children teacher much picture watch

r — read really programme arrive sorry married write wrong

silent 'r' — are sure here work garden person there yesterday upstairs near

ʒ — unusual usually revision garage

θ — three think thanks Thursday thousand birthday bath fourth

p — put people paper expensive cup stamp apple happy

l — low light little slow help pencil small spell

Quicktest 1

Files 1 to 3

Grammar

One of these sentences is wrong. Circle the right sentence.

Example a Where he's from?
           b Where's he from?

1. a Is a / b It's a — video camera.

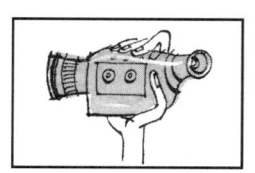

2. Bill and Nancy a isn't / b aren't very happy.

3. a Are you French? / b Are you Frenchs? — Yes, we are.

4. Do you speak German? a Yes, I speak. / b Yes, I do.

5. Would you like a drink? No, nothing for me, a please. / b thanks.

6. a He haves / b He has — two children.

7. What are a these? / b those?

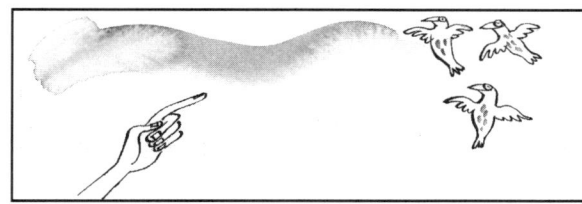

8. The birds are 
   a on the table and the cat's next to the table.
   b in the table and the cat's under the table.

9. a I'm not / b I don't — smoke.

10. What do you do? a I'm an engineer. / b I'm engineer.

11. a How much / b How many — is that? £4.50, please.

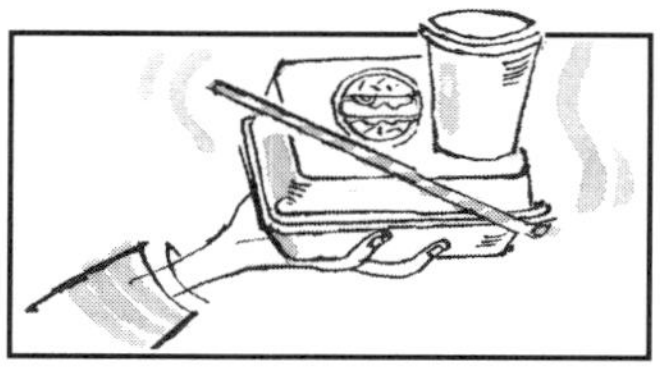

12. a Does / b Do — Liz live in a flat?

13. a No, she don't. She live / b No, she doesn't. She lives — in a house.

14. a Can you drive? / b Can you to drive? — No, I can't.

15. What's the time in Sydney?
    a It's ten to four.
    b It's ten past four.

16. a At what time opens the bank?
    b What time does the bank open?

Vocabulary

Which word is different? Circle it.

Example Tuesday Wednesday **February** Saturday

17. Spanish   Italy   France   Germany
18. journalist   job   lawyer   nurse
19. listen   read   pen   write
20. at   in   on   an
21. when   who   how   after
22. phones   address   names   papers
23. hour   arrive   second   minute
24. third   fifth   seven   ninth
25. they   his   her   your

Total 25

Quicktest 2

Files 4 and 5

Grammar

Two of these sentences are wrong. Circle the right one.

| Example | How old | a has he?
b is he?
c has he got? |

1. We all live in
   - a a yellow submarine.
   - b yellow submarine.
   - c a submarine yellow.

2. Aunt Mary is
   - a the sister my mother.
   - b my sister's mother.
   - c my mother's sister.

3. Excuse me. Where can we wash
   - a their
   - b our
   - c your

   hands?

4.
   - a Has you a car?
   - b Have you got a car?
   - c Do you have car?

   Yes, I have.

5. They haven't got
   - a some
   - b any
   - c a

   friends in the UK.

6. I love
   - a listening to music.
   - b listen to the music.
   - c listening music.

7.
   - a Could I
   - b I could
   - c I can

   have an envelope, please?

8. What time
   - a Tim goes to work?
   - b does Tim go to the work?
   - c does Tim go to work?

9.
   - a She no has
   - b She doesn't have
   - c She don't have

   cereal for breakfast.

10. How do they get to class?
    - a They walk.
    - b They go in car.
    - c They go on bus.

11.
    - a We drive always
    - b We always drive
    - c Always we drive

    to the supermarket.

12. I go to the theatre
    - a one
    - b twice
    - c three

    times a year.

13. Kim often goes
    - a away
    - b to
    - c out

    the cinema.

14.
    - a I'd like a
    - b I like a
    - c I like

    bottle of water, please.

15. He gets up and
    - a then
    - b after
    - c before

    he has a shower.

16. Tanya works
    - a at
    - b from
    - c of

    9.00 until 5.30.

Vocabulary

Which word is different in each group? Circle it.

| Example | a | an | **any** | the |

17. a hundred   a number   a thousand   a million
18. under   between   some   near
19. get   love   hate   takes
20. children   man   parents   women
21. how often   have got   which   how much
22. once   third   second   first
23. easy   fast   long   behind
24. restaurant   starter   main course   dessert
25. its   our   their   he

Total ☐ 25

84

Quicktest 3

Files 6 and 7

Grammar

Two of these sentences are wrong. Circle the right one.

Example Why
- a it did you do?
- b you did it?
- **(c)** did you do it?

1 What do you think of the Beatles?
I like
- a it.
- b him.
- c them.

2
- a There are
- b There's
- c They're

some chairs in this room.

3 Were you at home last night?
- a Yes, I were.
- b Yes, I was.
- c Yes, we was.

4 Sam's children were
- a in
- b at
- c to

the living-room.

5 There weren't
- a some
- b any
- c the

mushrooms.

6 What time
- a the first train leaves?
- b leaves the first train?
- c does the first train leave?

7 How old
- a is
- b has
- c have

your flat?

8
- a Did you have
- b Did you had
- c Had you

breakfast this morning?

9 He didn't
- a be
- b went
- c go

out last night.

10
- a I studied
- b I studed
- c I studyed

history at university.

11 30th March =
- a the third of March
- b the thirteenth of March
- c the thirtieth of March

12 Our son was born
- a twenty days before.
- b twenty days ago.
- c there are twenty days.

13
- a Can you tell me the where to the station, please?
- b Could you tell me the way to the station, please?
- c Could you tell the way to the station, please?

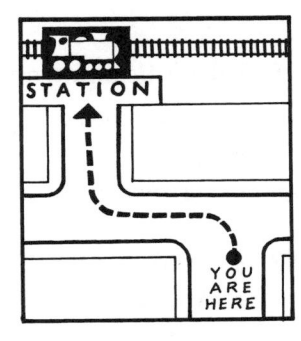

14
- a Yes. Go straight ahead. Turn left, then turn right.
- b Yes. Turn left. Go straight ahead, then turn right.
- c Yes. Turn right. Go straight ahead, then turn left.

15
- a What time
- b Who
- c How long

did you stay in Benidorm?

16 We visited the Louvre
- a the last year.
- b last year.
- c on 1994.

Vocabulary

Which word is different? Circle it.

Example why **(because)** which how many

17 in   at   then   to
18 great   fantastic   lovely   awful
19 carpet   cook   mirror   fridge
20 February   Thursday   June   November
21 twentieth   twenty-one   twenty-two   twenty-three
22 went   had   saw   worked
23 changed   typed   need   tried
24 usually   walk   always   often
25 her   us   him   they

Total ☐ 25

Quicktest 4

Files 8 and 9

Grammar

Two of these sentences are wrong. Circle the right one.

Example We a not working today.
           b aren't working today.
           c don't working today.

1 What's he doing now?
   a He watches
   b He's watch   TV again!
   c He's watching

2 a Do they
   b Are they   usually eat at 7.00?
   c Does they

3 Joanna's wearing
   a black shoes.
   b a black shoes.
   c shoes black.

4 a How long
   b How often   do you buy new clothes?
   c How many

5 a What do
   b What are   you going to do this summer?
   c What's

6 a We aren't
   b We don't   going to buy a new car.
   c We not

7 a It was rain
   b It's rained last night.
   c It rained

8 I'm sorry. It's engaged.
   Don't worry, a I call
                 b I'll call   back later.
                 c I am call

9 Is your brother
   a biger
   b more big   than you?
   c bigger

10 Elephants are
   a heavier than
   b heavy than   camels.
   c more heavy than

11 Do you think it's
   a going to be
   b be   all right?
   c being

12 Oliver's eating very
   a quickly.
   b quick.
   c fastly.

13 Naomi plays
   a chess very good.
   b chess very well.
   c very well chess.

14 We haven't got
   a a
   b some   meat.
   c any

15 a How many milk
   b How much milk   would you like?
   c How much milks

Vocabulary

Which word is different? Circle it.

Example **get** spoke said took

16 can't isn't wasn't doesn't
17 coat dress socks cases
18 opposite between behind left
19 sing running playing having
20 Then After that So Who
21 younger horrible worse more comfortable
22 quickly luckily easy well
23 yesterday today tomorrow next
24 oil potato sugar rice
25 carton kilo packet tin

Total [ ] 25

Grammar words

		Examples
☐	adjective	big, yellow
☐	adverb	quickly, happily
☐	adverb of frequency	always, usually
☐	article	a / an, the
☐	auxiliary (verb)	do, did, can.
☐	comparative adjective	older, more difficult
☐	consonant	b, c, d, f, g
☐	contraction	I'm, you're, isn't
☐	infinitive (verb)	be, go (= the dictionary form of a verb)
☐	-ing form	reading, cycling
☐	negative	−
☐	noun (singular)	apple, bus
☐	noun (plural)	apples, buses
☐	positive	+
☐	preposition	from, in, on
☐	pronoun	I, you, he
☐	question	What?, Where?
☐	short answer	✓ ✗ Yes, I am., No, we don't.
☐	stress	happy, English
☐	tense	present, past, future
☐	verb	get, have, look
☐	vowel	a, e, i, o, u

Punctuation

☐	apostrophe '	it's, Jenny's, can't
☐	capital letter	A, B, C
☐	comma ,	a cat, a dog, a bird
☐	full stop .	Come on., Let's go.
☐	question mark ?	When?, How are you?
☐	small letter	a, b, c

Contractions file

1 No contraction in + short answers:
   Yes, I **am**.   NOT   ~~Yes, I'm.~~
   Yes, we **have**. NOT   ~~Yes, we've.~~

2 Contraction in − short answers:
   No, **I'm** not.   No, we **haven't**.

3 Only contract *are* with *we / you / they*:
   we**'re** / you**'re** / they**'re**

   Where **are**   NOT   ~~Where're~~
   What **are**   NOT   ~~What're~~
   There **are**   NOT   ~~There're~~

4 No contraction with *it* at the end of a sentence:
   Where's the station?
   BUT   Where is **it**?   NOT   ~~Where's it?~~
   What's this? **What's** the time?
   BUT   What is **it**?   NOT   ~~What's it?~~

A Complete the contractions.

'm	=	am
's	=	is
're	=	are
n't	=	_____
isn't	=	is not
aren't	=	_____ _____
Let's	=	Let us
don't	=	_____
doesn't	=	does not
can't	=	_____
haven't	=	have not
've	=	_____
hasn't	=	_____ _____
's got	=	has got

B Complete the contractions.

I'd like	=	I would like
there's	=	_____ _____
wasn't	=	_____ _____
weren't	=	_____ _____
didn't	=	_____ _____
couldn't	=	_____ _____
I'll have	=	I _____ _____

Oxford University Press
Great Clarendon Street, Oxford OX2 6DP

Oxford New York
Auckland Bangkok Buenos Aires Cape Town
Chennai Dar es Salaam Delhi Hong Kong Istanbul
Karachi Kolkata Kuala Lumpur Madrid Melbourne
Mexico City Mumbai Nairobi São Paulo Shanghai
Taipei Tokyo Toronto

OXFORD and OXFORD ENGLISH
are trade marks of Oxford University Press

ISBN 0 19 436860 2

© Oxford University Press 2000

Database right Oxford University Press (maker)

First published 2000
Seventh impression 2003

No unauthorized photocopying

All rights reserved. No part of this publication may be reproduced, stored in a retrieval system, or transmitted, in any form or by any means, without the prior permission in writing of Oxford University Press, or as expressly permitted by law, or under terms agreed with the appropriate reprographics rights organization. Enquiries concerning reproduction outside the scope of the above should be sent to the ELT Rights Department, Oxford University Press, at the address above

You must not circulate this book in any other binding or cover and you must impose this same condition on any acquirer

Any websites referred to in this publication are in the public domain and their addresses are provided by Oxford University Press for information only. Oxford University Press disclaims any responsibility for the content.

Origination by Blenheim Colour, Eynsham, Oxford

Printed in China

Acknowledgements

Illustrations by:

Rowan Barnes Murphy
Neil Gower
Nick Hardcastle
Lotty
Ellis Nadler
OUP Technical Graphics Department
Alastair Taylor

Studio photography by:

Stephen Oliver

Location photography by:

John Walmsley

Thanks to the following for their help with photography:

The Eckersley School of English, Oxford
Barclays Bank Plc

The publishers would like to thank the following for permission to reproduce photographs:

Colorific Library
Edinburgh Library
Hulton Deutsch
Rex Features
Science Photo Library
Sygma Ltd
Telegraph Colour Library
Tony Stone Images
John Walmsley

We would also like to thank Johnny Hart and Creators Syndicate, Inc. for their kind permission to reproduce the Wizard of Id cartoon.

Design by Amanda Goodridge